Praise for *Getting to Like*:

"Sharing your story is like breathing oxygen in the digital age. It is a must for a professional to thrive. Your personal brand is the key to opening the gates to the right partners, collaborations, and growth opportunities. Jeremy and Ali's book *Getting to Like* gives you all the tools you need to find your authentic voice and figure out how to share it. I more than liked the book, I loved it. You will too."

—Michael TS Lindenmayer, coauthor of *Art's Principles*

"Zagat and Goldman have created a masterclass in personal branding. As approachable as the 'Dummy' series but with the tone and smarts of TED, *Getting to Like* provides readers with the reasons why building your personal brand should be as tantamount as a basic education and delivers a practical framework for developing and maintaining it. This book should be required reading for professionals and students alike, especially given just how dominating social media is in today's world."

—Michael Barber, founder, Barber & Hewitt

"In an age when technological change has radically transformed the marketplace, nothing is more important for the young and ambitious to understand than that success depends upon branding, both in the personal profile one projects to the world and in the business image the world sees. In *Getting to Like*, the landscape of this new world and the primacy of branding is described with the clarity and urgency it requires. Read this book and succeed!"

— Frédéric Fekkai, celebrity hairstylist and beauty legend

"Personal branding will have a significant impact on your professional opportunities throughout the career cycle. If you fail to gain visibility you will become lost in the crowd of nameless profiles. Now more than ever, you must establish your unique digital identity, and build meaningful relationships with your audience. I found *Getting to Like* to be a practical, actionable primer to help you stay one or two steps ahead of the curve—and your competition."

—Matt Britton, author of best-selling *YouthNation* and founder and CEO, MRY

Getting
to
Like

**HOW TO BOOST YOUR PERSONAL AND
PROFESSIONAL BRAND
TO EXPAND OPPORTUNITIES, GROW YOUR BUSINESS,
AND ACHIEVE FINANCIAL SUCCESS**

Jeremy Goldman and Ali B. Zagat

CAREER
PRESS

Wayne, NJ

GETTING TO LIKE
EDITED BY ROGER SHEETY
TYPESET BY KARA KUMPEL
Cover design by Brian Moore
Printed in the U.S.A.

To order this title, please call toll-free 1-800-CAREER-1 (NJ and Canada: 201-848-0310) to order using VISA or MasterCard, or for further information on books from Career Press.

The Career Press, Inc.
12 Parish Drive
Wayne, NJ 07470
www.careerpress.com

Library of Congress Cataloging-in-Publication Data

CIP Data Available Upon Request.

Acknowledgments

There are so many people to thank that we're sure to forget someone and get in trouble. But we'll try anyway!

First off, we'd like to thank our spouses, John and Victoria. John is Ali's, by the by. Our families, in general, are pretty great and deserve acknowledgment for their incredible ongoing support, love, and understanding of our weird writing schedules.

We also want to thank our secret digital networking group, Mosaic. It's a referral-based group of supportive digital marketers and other professionals who are invested in one another's success. We'd especially like to thank Katie Keating, Lauren DeGeorge, Abby Whitmer, Matthew Capala, Esther Brown, Carly Fink, Vie Quartuccio, Sonya Magett, Leiti Hsu, and Diane Rankin, who chimed in when we were looking for names for the book you're now reading.

A quick shout-out to Grind, the amazing coworking space in New York City that hosted many of our meet-ups, interviews, marathon writing/editing sessions, and occasional disco naps. We couldn't have done it without you (and your copious supplies of coffee).

But the #1 acknowledgment we have to give is our third team member, Luke Robbins. We were looking for an intern when we met Luke, who had recently graduated from the University of Michigan. We quickly found that Luke is a stellar natural writer with great storytelling skills. Frankly, we wouldn't be surprised if he surpassed us. You can find him on Twitter @LukeBRobbins. He writes in quite a few different places and maintains a blog at Concerningwriters.com.

Contents

Introduction

Why Does Personal Branding Matter? And Why Should You Be Reading This?

While running for president of the United States in 2012, Mitt Romney famously said: "Corporations are people, my friends." Actually, we think the converse is true: People, in a sense, are corporations. Until recently, we thought that only companies had brand identities. That is, until we started thinking of celebrities—such as Kim Kardashian, Beyoncé, or Donald Trump—as having them, too. Today, we're increasingly aware that each individual's reputation and attributes constitute someone's unique personal brand.

Just like household name brands, you have characteristics that define you: ways that you think of yourself and ways that others think of you. Your personal brand is made up of thousands of choices and opinions, from the simple to the complex. Everyone you've ever met has formed opinions about you. You may not be aware of your brand, and that means it might not be the best, most accurate representation of who you are and what you're capable of. Effective personal branding isn't about putting on a show or figuring out how to do as little work as possible while getting the most financial reward. Life is too short not to be the best possible version of yourself.

So, who needs to care about personal branding, anyway? Is it really *that* important?

The short answers to these two questions are a) Virtually everyone, and b) Yes, it is. How people see you matters. This is a fundamental truth of being a human being.

You have a brand just as much as you have a reputation. Are you the life of the party? Well, that's part of your brand. Do you tend to take control in a key business meeting? That's part of your brand, too. Are you prone to making bad jokes when you're nervous? That's part of your br—well, you get the picture.

So let's talk about some potential situations you may be facing right now. You might be trying to:

- 👍 Raise your profile in general, by getting better known for the skills that you have.
- 👍 Launch your own brand or startup from scratch, and know you'll have to be the best version of yourself for it to succeed.
- 👍 Increase your profile to market your brand to prospective clients.
- 👍 Digitally connect with your existing customers to figure out what they think, what they like, and how to better satisfy their needs.

Personal branding can help you accomplish all of these things. So when do you need to look into refining your personal brand? Here are some situations you might be facing:

- 👍 Your career is just starting out and you're concerned that people don't know what you're capable of.
- 👍 You're looking to grow your influence in your existing company and move up through the ranks, but something about your reputation is stopping you from getting there.

- You're trying to move from one area of your company to another.

- You're trying to change careers entirely and want to convince others that your existing skill set will be an asset, not a drawback.

- You've been laid off from a job and need to ensure that you're in the best possible position to land a new job—the right new job—in as short a time as possible.

- You're going back to the workforce after taking time off; perhaps after having children; perhaps re-entering the workforce after retirement.

So, why did we decide to write this book together and help others master their personal brands? For the last 15 years, Jeremy has been doing just that. After college, he started a Website development firm, which led to a career managing e-commerce for a number of international beauty brands. This led him to write *Going Social* and launch Firebrand Group, a digital consultancy focused on building powerful brands through marketing, visual branding, and innovation.

Ali knows the importance of personal branding first-hand. She started out working at Thomson Reuters editing financial treatises (sexy, right?) before rebranding herself and joining the fast-paced e-commerce world with Fab.com. At Fab, Ali wrote sales copy, product copy, and social content, including some of the site's highest-trafficked pieces ever. Ali got a taste for being on the other side of the editor's desk while helping Jeremy prepare *Going Social* for publication. After working at Amazon in a managerial capacity, she is now a copywriter at a branding agency and helps companies and entrepreneurs connect with their audiences. She practically (if not literally) lives and breathes branding, and sees the importance of having a strong brand identity reinforced every day.

In addition to being an important read, we aim to make this an interesting one as well. We'll be accomplishing this with case studies and stories from many first-hand accounts of personal branding successes—and pitfalls—from luminaries such as:

- ☝ Founder and CEO of Bezar (and cofounder of Fab), Bradford Shellhammer.
- ☝ Army veteran turned actor Melvin Kearney.
- ☝ Content marketer Jason Miller.
- ☝ *Crain's New York* 40 Under 40 member Anuj Desai.
- ☝ Author and television personality Andrea Syrtash.
- ☝ Adam Cohen, founder of the famous *DaDa Rocks* blog.

All of these personal branding standouts have learned an important lesson: If you don't acknowledge (or choose not to tailor the presentation of) your brand, people will draw their own conclusions.

Many people like to keep their head down and focus on the day-to-day operations of their job. You're entirely welcome to just focus on your "real" work, as opposed to also focusing on the branding work we advocate in this book. But why settle for that, given how important your career is to you? Is there really a benefit to not presenting yourself well? Look at where you are in your career. Is this where you want to be? If you've picked up this book, there's a decent chance you've already asked yourself that very question.

Life is too short to do a job you're not passionate about—or worse, that you might outright hate. You don't want to get stuck in a career that doesn't fulfill you or play to your strengths, do you? It's very important for each one of us to explore whether we're doing all that we can to have the best possible professional lives.

A quick word on our title, *Getting to Like*. Why? Just because we say "like" does not mean we're referring to Facebook Likes. In fact, you may find that Facebook isn't the ideal place to build your personal brand. That's completely fine! As a matter of fact, Likes on Facebook are hardly the barometer for success, as we'll talk about later. We're talking about the overall concepts of getting people to like you by standing for something, being compelling, and building the best possible version of you. This book is about getting people to "like" you in a way that will build you into the standout we know you're capable of being.

Coming up, we'll make a case for the importance of personal branding, and present compelling reasons for how defining your brand identity will only become more important in the decade ahead. We'll examine the social trends shaping today's marketplace, and highlight one of the biggest trends that you should be aware of: the growth of freelance culture. As more professionals transition out of full-time roles at larger companies, you'll need to establish and promote yourself competitively if you want to improve your earning potential and quality of life.

Next, you'll learn how to lay the groundwork for a compelling personal brand. To do this, we'll help you develop (or streamline) your personal brand statement. We'll also help you identify key traits to emphasize, and take you through some exercises to define your strengths and convey them in a succinct, compelling manner. Think of this as your elevator pitch: a mission statement for yourself, your business, and everything you hope to achieve. People are busy, and your potential clients and audience will want to know who they're dealing with. A strong personal brand statement can help them decide to work with you, follow you, and make your brand part of their life.

Now you have a compelling brand statement. But if no one ever hears your voice or what you have to add to the professional world, does it really matter? We don't think anyone will disagree if we say that the most efficient place to broadcast your brand is through digital and social platforms. So we'll analyze the strengths and weaknesses of the three most common forms of content shared through those channels: text, photos, and video. We'll help you determine which are most appropriate for you, and share some strategies for increasing your proficiency in your medium of choice.

After that, we'll dive into the most popular digital and social channels for sharing content from those you might know (LinkedIn, Facebook, Twitter, Pinterest, Instagram, Snapchat) to those you might not recognize. We'll cover how to determine which platforms are the right ones for you—LinkedIn and Twitter are favorites of ours for building strong brands—and how many you can effectively use without spreading your focus too thin. From there, we'll show you how to best leverage the potential of those channels to grow your brand. After all, although you can and should promote your brand on several different channels, you wouldn't share the exact thoughts on Pinterest as you would on LinkedIn, right? You would? Uh-oh.

Building a digital presence is important, but we would never advocate for only engaging virtually and leaving the "real world" behind. From national conferences to local networking events, you have the opportunity to be the face of your brand and demonstrate how you're the living, breathing embodiment of everything you've been saying digitally. That's why we'll move the focus offline to explore the importance of "real life," face-to-face interactions and how personally representing your brand can be a valuable part of your branding strategy.

Being authentic has always been important, and today's culture demands it even more than in the past. We'll examine our society's obsession with authenticity, and how you may be hurting your brand by pursuing this quality for its own sake. We'll also discuss the tug of war between authenticity and self-editing. As a compelling storyteller, how should you best pick and choose what you share?

And speaking of authenticity, we all have different facets of our lives that sometimes seem difficult to reconcile. Think of how you might be known as an avid comic book collector, yet at the same time you're a buttoned-up financial consultant. We'll help you reconcile inconsistencies and even contradictions in your personal brand, uniting previous iterations of your identity and highlighting the different facets of your personality in a positive manner.

Given that branding, by definition, can't operate in a vacuum, it's crucial to understand how others view your personal brand.

We'll also cover the importance of feedback (both reactive and proactive). And not just any feedback—impressions and opinions you can actually use to improve and refine your brand. We'll show you how to turn your connections into an expert panel of brand analysts in order to solicit constructive criticism, and how to interpret and apply your findings.

After all the hard work you've done, your brand should feel rock solid. Although even seasoned branding experts have found that it's all too easy to get off topic, that doesn't mean it's any less important to maintain directional control. We'll highlight the difference between "ready, aim, fire" and "ready, fire, aim" to help you tailor the presentation of your brand to keep your messaging on target.

No matter how conscientious you are of your brand, and despite your most diligent efforts to remain on track, you may look at yourself and realize your brand is in dire need of repair. We'll outline how to identify when you're in this type of situation, and when you may have to think about reinventing yourself. Whether you need to retarget or do some damage control, we'll guide you through the process.

Finally, you've made it to the point where you're done with personal branding forever, and you're all set until you die. Wait, what's that? You have to manage your personal brand and do upkeep on an ongoing basis? Yes, you do. We've come up with a few techniques to help you plan the most time-effective strategy for conducting continuous brand maintenance and fine-tuning, so that your digital and in-person presentation are always the most up-to-date reflection of your skills, strengths, and passions.

We've noticed through our combined years of experience that there are some vital skills and traits many successful entrepreneurs and freelancers have in common. We call this set "how to be awesome." If you feel like you're not awesome yet, don't despair. It's something that every professional works hard to develop, and then refines and hones with time, again and again. Becoming awesome is a journey, not a destination, so we'll go over this ongoing process in great detail.

You probably have a sense of this already, but mastering and maintaining your personal brand is a pretty significant undertaking. It takes time and effort, and even the smartest, savviest people out there go through some trial and error before they figure out what works for them and what doesn't. So what can you do to build your personal brand as smoothly as possible? That's what this book is for: helping you become focused, so you can eliminate distractions and identify what will get you where you need to go, versus what will delay or divert you. And if you have any questions along the way, even in the middle of reading this book—especially in the middle of reading this book!—ask us. We'll be monitoring #GtoL on Twitter to respond to our readers. Please don't hesitate to reach out at any time.

So, what are you waiting for? Let's get to it.

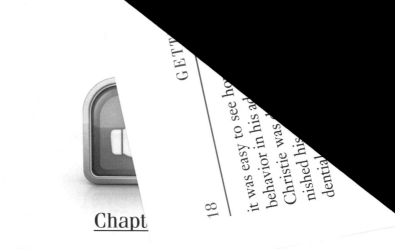

it was easy to see ho
behavior in his a
Christie was
nished his
dential

Chapt

Who Needs to ⌐⌐⌐ About Personal Branding?

Controlling Your Personal Brand

In early 2014, New Jersey Governor Chris Christie was the consensus choice as the most eligible prospective candidate for the 2016 Republican presidential nomination. Christie was known as a brash, outspoken truth-teller, the kind of guy who didn't play games in the same manner as most politicians. To many, he was a breath of fresh air. But then something happened. A few lanes of traffic had been closed on the George Washington Bridge, which was inconvenient but seemingly minor. During the course of the next few months, the media broke a major scandal: What had appeared to be a random street closure was actually an act of political retaliation against Fort Lee's mayor, who had not supported Christie's reelection for governor. Members of the Christie administration had deliberately closed these lanes to create traffic in the town of Fort Lee. Christie's ruthlessness and aggressive nature was suddenly seen in a new light;

w his aggressive brand encouraged this type of
ministration. Although there was never proof that
irectly involved in the lane closures, the scandal tar-
personal brand and hurt his chances of getting the presi-
nomination.

Just like Christie, you have a personal brand. In fact, every professional has one, regardless of whether they have done any work
to develop it or not. If you don't continuously work on your brand,
you're not going to be in control of the story. Rather than being defined on your own terms, you'll be defined by others.

You might not have any aspirations for public office, but you can
still learn from the Christie example. When your brand is tied to
your career prospects and professional trajectory, it's important to
make sure how you represent yourself translates into others' perceptions of you.

The idea that hard work *alone* will get you ahead has been thoroughly discredited. When it comes to your career, perceptions matter. You want both relevant professionals in your field and the general population to be able to recognize your abilities so that you can
get the opportunities you deserve.

The Importance of Brands

Everyone is his or her own brand. You need to have what it takes
to be the CEO of "Me, Incorporated." Everything from the shoes
that you wear to the coffee travel mug you carry can be a part of
your brand. Whatever your age or position or the business you're
in, it's necessary to understand the importance of branding. To be in
business today, you have to be head marketer for your own personal
brand.

Anyone and anything can be a brand that's worthy of getting
attention. To big companies, this is a fundamental principle. Brands
encompass all kinds of products and services, and every company,
from accounting firms to sneaker makers, is working to escape the

narrow confines of its category and become a brand that's surrounded by buzz.

Personal Branding's Rising Importance

Personal branding is especially crucial for the current generation of workers, the most professionally mobile workforce yet. As a group, we're more likely to move from one job to another in quick succession, whether to improve salary, to seek better working conditions, or because we're forced out by a cost-cutting layoff. Many workers also hold down several jobs at once. You may have heard stories from your parents or grandparents of lifetime careers at one firm, but the days of investing 40-plus years at any one company are long gone. Through the course of their careers, most of today's professionals will change companies, transition between completely different careers, and be hired by companies as consultants or freelance workers. Establishing a strong personal brand provides a range of opportunities whenever it's time to move on, allowing you to make those transitions smoothly.

Jeanne Meister, the renowned enterprise learning consultant, wrote a piece entitled "Job Hopping Is the New Normal for Millennials." As part of a response to a reader's comment, she said, "…job hopping is the new black. Employers see a downside if candidates stay at a company for longer than 10 years, and want to know why."[1] Though being a long-term employee has had positive connotations in the past, employers today may wonder if you just weren't ambitious enough to look for other opportunities. You don't want anyone to think that you got too comfortable and never tried to push yourself. So if you've been at your job for longer than 10 years, take note. You may have thought it was a sign of loyalty, but it may be perceived as a career liability.

It's now standard to see high levels of job turnover. This makes changing companies more acceptable, which in turn only begets greater job turnover. The Future Workplace "Multiple Generations @ Work" survey found that 91 percent of Millennials—those born between 1977 and 1997—expect to stay in a job for less than three years.[2] That equates to 15 to 20 different jobs through the course of a single professional's working life.

But it's not just younger individuals who need to think about their personal brand; those who are already established in their careers should be thinking about it as well. An April 2014 Gallup report found that "Americans' average self-reported age of retirement has slowly moved upward: the average retirement age was 57 in 1993, but the average age at which non-retired Americans now expect to retire is 66."[3]

This trend of working later in life isn't likely to reverse itself anytime soon; if anything, it might accelerate. Often it's by necessity, as those who leave the workforce live longer lives and find that Social Security just won't cut it. Now that older Americans are working longer, they're competing with people who are up to four or five decades younger, which necessitates the ability to stay vital, reinvent their professional identity, and remain competitive in the marketplace. And beyond pure economic necessity, many people are choosing to work rather than retire, finding that staying active makes them feel more fulfilled. This concept is even the theme of *The Intern*, a 2015 film starring Robert De Niro and Anne Hathaway. De Niro plays a 70-year-old former executive who gets bored with retirement and applies to a senior citizen intern program at Anne Hathaway's character's firm.

Given the increasing trend toward transitioning between different companies and career paths, simply defining yourself by your job (for example, "Ali is a writer") can paint you into a corner or lead you down a professional dead end. For a more advantageous and flexible approach, highlight the qualities you've honed (for example, "Ali is adaptable and skilled in content creation") that will make you a valuable asset across multiple industries. Ali once interviewed for a position she was extremely interested in, and spoke enthusiastically about her background as a writer—only to find that the company was looking to hire someone with extensive experience creating video scripts. If she had been a little less narrow in her definition, she might have had a better shot at getting the role. Similarly, although you may have the ability to look at your previous career in sales and see that you would be able to succeed in logistics, that won't be apparent to everybody you're interviewing with. If you're thinking of transitioning between industries, it is important to develop your personal brand so that people understand how your previous achievements in one field tie into the successes you feel you can accomplish in another. It's all part of marketing yourself successfully.

Even if you stay within the same industry—or the same company—for a long time, you're likely to have to reinvent your professional self in order to stay relevant. For example, a marketer who was predominantly focused on developing print advertising with a secondary focus on digital marketing has likely had to reinvent herself during the last few years.

That's what Dina Rosenbloom had to do after her employer, Jurlique, went belly-up. Though Rosenbloom, a beauty veteran, had managed the Web functions at some of her previous companies, she largely relied on digital subject matter experts. As part of rebranding herself, she not only emphasized her digital experience more than before, but also worked to increase her digital aptitude. She took some additional classes in her spare time, volunteered to spearhead digital projects for nonprofits, and asked digital marketers within her network for advice. Her expanded knowledge of digital, social, and mobile spheres has paid large dividends in helping her land at the right job: She's currently VP of marketing at International Cosmetics and Perfumes, a beauty conglomerate responsible for both the digital and traditional marketing of a number of prestige beauty brands. Increasingly, those who find long-term career success have similar stories.

Although personal branding is incredibly important to a brand-side employee such as Rosenbloom, it's arguably even more important to long-term or career freelancers. Increasingly, talented professionals are forming their own individual businesses instead of working in one role for one company, putting the big company in the role of client rather than employer.

According to *The Intuit 2020 Report*, a 2010 study designed to look at the next decade, more than 40 percent of the U.S. workforce—more than 60 million workers—will be "contingent workers" or free agents. Moreover, 80 percent of large corporations plan to substantially increase their usage of permanent freelancers, in part so that they don't have to provide health insurance (according to your cynical authors). Need more convincing? The Bureau of Labor Statistics found that the number of temporary employees jumped 29 percent between 2009 and 2012. On average, temporary workers comprised 22 percent of the workforce among the 200 largest companies in the U.S.

By all accounts, this number continues to rise. Workers across multiple industries are realizing that they can support themselves without a full-time place of employment.[4] But if you go the permanent freelance route, your personal brand *is* your corporate brand. How effectively you present that brand directly affects your ability to pay the bills. In many ways, personal branding will improve your earning potential and quality of life. Call us crazy, but that's a pretty good thing to aim for.

The Impact of Technology and Globalization

Technology has had a major impact on globalization, allowing companies, regardless of size, to do business with customers, start partnerships, and open up offices all over the world. Coupled with the growth of digital and social media, globalization has made personal branding more important than ever. Your prospective audience does not just consist of your local network; it might consist of *more than a billion individuals*. After all, as of April 2014, the Internet at large had more than 2.4 billion users total, including 255 million monthly active Twitter users, and 300 million registered LinkedIn users. The possibilities for building connections and making your name known are now virtually limitless.

Globalization can be perceived as a positive or a negative. If you put in the work to develop a strong brand presence, your reputation can precede you when you're doing work on an international scale.

Your new business partners in South Korea can look you up on LinkedIn, view your personal Website, and follow you on Twitter, all to get a sense of you and help strengthen their relationship with you. Of course, then they're also privy to any inadvertent slip-ups you might make—which we'll cover later on.

Getting Over the Discomfort of Personal Branding

As we began the process of finding people to interview and asking them about their approach to personal branding, it brought up ideas about artificiality and constructed nature. We realized that asking people how they created their public image might make them uncomfortable, because "revealing" their methods might make the whole process seem fabricated and dishonest. In order to get over this feeling, you need to believe in what you're saying.

If you asked Stephen Fry, the renowned English comedian, actor, writer, and activist, how he manages to seem so witty and knowledgeable, he would tell you (much more eloquently than we could) that he does so by *being* witty and knowledgeable. This is a useful idea to keep in mind as you ask yourself: What makes top-quality personal branding stand out? It is this feeling of authenticity, the belief that what you're putting forward is genuine and honest. The "branding" part of this is simply your ability to display those skills and attributes.

Striking Out on Your Own

The decision to leave an established company and work for yourself can be exhilarating, but also ridiculously frightening. It's more comfortable to have the security of a well-known, entrenched company behind you, so you can leverage its reputation. But sometimes it's in your best interests to be bold and leave for new horizons. If you have an idea about how to improve a product, do a job better, or take an idea in a new direction, then starting your own business might make the most sense for you.

It goes without saying, but just in case: Never bad-mouth your old company or criticize how they operate. You never know; they might become your client one day.

Staking Out Unique Turf

Your personal brand will form as you carve out your niche. We call this ability to stand out from the crowd *managed distinction*, and it will be instrumental in helping you position yourself as not only an expert in your field, but one with a unique background, skill set, and perspective. Don't try to blend in or do what everyone else is doing. When is it time to be memorable in your career? Always.

No matter how smart and diligent you are, there are plenty of people out there who are just as intelligent as you and work as hard as you do. The rise of the Internet has put many tools at your competitors' disposal, helping them to position themselves to their best advantage. What's the good news? You, too, have access to these tools. In fact, if you're reading this book, you have better access than many people do. A carefully crafted personal brand gives you an edge over your competition. Carving out a distinct social niche can help you both define and reach your audience.

Being a unique brand makes you less replaceable. Your best approach is to make your content fun, attention-grabbing, and inspired. The consequences of being boring are worse than those of offending a few people. In fact, there's nothing wrong with being a contrarian in your views, and in many cases, that can help separate you from the rest of the pack. You shouldn't be provocative for the sake of it, but if you truly have an opposing point of view, it would benefit you to share it. Similarly, don't stand out by creating a unique yet inauthentic persona. Your brand is something that you'll have to stand behind for a long time. Don't make the mistake of assuming an identity that you can't maintain. As the saying goes, "Be yourself. Everyone else is already taken."

Your first objective is to find a tone for communicating with your audience—one that will distinguish your brand from the competition. One of the most powerful ways to connect with a specific group is to use unique language, a kind of unifying lingo that both helps the members of the community to identify each other and reinforces community bonds. When you meet people in person, you make connections by sharing what's noteworthy about yourself; those features help define you. When you define your social voice and approach, think of what makes you stand out from others. If you sound like everyone else, you have a much greater chance of being overlooked or forgotten.

The Fat Jew

Would you choose the moniker of "The Fat Jew"? It doesn't exactly sound like the result of careful planning, right? But for Josh Ostrovsky, maintaining this alter ego is performance art, and something he has to reconcile with his personal life. This is not to say that he doesn't embody the traits that made his character so popular—it would be nearly impossible to fake something so ostentatious—but there's still a dial he has to turn up or down for each situation. When he posted a picture of himself on Instagram at Cannes Film Festival, pouring two bottles of rosé champagne onto his tux, it's safe to say that the dial was turned pretty far up.

But that's Instagram. As we discussed earlier, it's kind of necessary to be loud on social media (to the point of semi-loveable obnoxiousness in Ostrovsky's case) if you want to be heard. But the issue is, that sort of personality does not work out so well in real life, where cartoonishness can become grating quite quickly. The same kind of antics that make The Fat Jew so popular on Instagram can make the polarizing Ostrovsky a bit much in person.

By playing such a loud character and toeing the line, Ostrovsky really has to be careful—people love to hate characters like this. So in Ostrovsky's case, harmlessness is a big factor in staying popular. In many cases, those who build their career on obnoxiousness include a healthy dose of putting others down for a laugh. But Ostrovsky is poking fun at himself.

Personal Branding Role Models

The business world is full of successful individuals who have become experts at building their own personal brands. Take Donny Deutsch, the advertising executive and television personality. Deutsch is the chairman of Deutsch Inc., a major advertising firm, which he sold to the Interpublic Group of Companies in 2000 for $265 million. He hosted the talk show *The Big Idea With Donny Deutsch*, appears as a regular guest on numerous talk shows, and has published several books largely focused on business success and motivation.

While we're on the subject of Donalds, what about Donald Trump? He's built an incredibly successful brand around his brash demeanor and personality. Although Trump's experience as a real estate magnate and businessperson is substantial, it's secondary to his reputation, which he has leveraged to sell television shows and clothing and, notably, enter the 2016 Presidential race as a Republican candidate.

Mika Brzezinski, cohost of MSNBC's *Morning Joe*, has built her brand around more than just her skills as a journalist; she is known for her dedication to physical and mental health, as well as the issue of balancing work and family, which many professional women must consistently maintain.

These individuals, among many others, have figured out that what they do and say directly ties into their personal brands and their ability to have successful careers. Once you've established your own distinctive personality, you have a greater ability to promote yourself as a "thought leader." Build upon what makes you unique. What special skills do you possess? What distinctive experiences have you had? Ali has her brown belt in the martial arts discipline of Krav Maga. Although this speaks to her dedication and perseverance, it doesn't sound like a resume-builder, right? Actually, including that information in her profile has sparked conversations with potential employers and clients, especially as Ali began creating more content for fitness brands.

How to Convey Your Message

Defining yourself professionally—whether by reinventing yourself or simply refining what you're already known for—is both an ongoing and a difficult process. This is true whether you are at the very beginning of your career or are well established; either way, you need to position yourself to your best advantage. Most people struggle with effectively communicating their story across social media and in real life. Here are three tips to attract an audience and keep them interested:

#1: Balance Transparency and Relevancy

How honest should you be when promoting your views, both on social media and in face-to-face conversations? Given the current near-obsession with authenticity, it's normal to be concerned that self-censoring might be viewed as inherently inauthentic. However, it's important to balance the need for authenticity with the desire to be audience-oriented; not everyone wants to hear every little detail about you. Your communication should be tailored to your current audience—friends will likely be much more tolerant of your #foodie posts than clients, unless you work in a relevant industry.

#2: First Impressions Truly Do Matter

You've probably heard that you only have seven seconds to make a strong first impression. So it would be hard to fault your audience for losing interest if you don't start out strong. That's why it's crucial to come right out of the gate with your most valuable and attention-grabbing thoughts—those that will leave a lasting impression in your audience's mind and appeal to their needs.

#3: Don't Put All Your Eggs in One Basket

It's easy to get caught up with one particular platform, but by neglecting others, you may be missing out on a substantial portion of your potential audience. In order to reach the widest range of prospects, it's useful to leverage different platforms and mechanisms, such as Facebook, Twitter, conferences, one-on-one meetings, and so forth. You don't want to spread yourself too thin; finding the right balance of variety and focus is key.

Putting It All Together

Everything you do communicates the value of your brand, from the way you handle yourself on the phone to how you respond to Facebook comments. It all becomes part of your brand, a combination of what you have to say, how well you say it, and your style. Do you have a command of whatever social platforms you're operating on, such as Twitter, LinkedIn, or others? Are you keeping everything short and to the point? Do you have a logo and/or business card that ties everything together and really hammers home who you are? In a crowded market, strong packaging will get you major brownie points.

This is especially true when word of mouth marketing is crucial. When people try too hard, the audience can tell, and those efforts look desperate. Instead, you have to try to be true to yourself, and put content out there that you're proud of. Your network of friends, clients, and customers will communicate who you are and your contributions to the market.

We've only scratched the surface so far, so let's get started with all the rest. Turn the page and we'll teach you how to develop your own shiny new personal brand statement.

Chapter 2

How to Lay the Groundwork for Branding Success

What Exactly Is My Brand, Anyway?

One of the most crucial steps for a personal brand is to justify its existence in the first place. If you had to make a case for your brand, how would you defend it?

This was the driving question that Adam Cohen faced when he founded *DaDa Rocks*, a blog dedicated to sharing his trials, triumphs, and tips for surviving fatherhood. Although *DaDa Rocks* is now an award-winning and well-known Website, when Adam was just starting out he had to ask himself: "Why should this blog exist, and what makes me the right guy to write it?"[1]

Adam found that the mom-blogger niche was pretty saturated, but "there wasn't anyone who could be the voice of a 'pro dad.' I wanted to read about someone who loves his kid and wife more than life itself, but is still having adventures." That type of voice didn't exist in the marketplace, so he decided to fill that void.

When you find yourself in a position in which you feel uniquely qualified to speak, you have to look to how you can provide for others. Adam felt isolated; when his child was 8 months old, none of his peers were parents yet, which helped him realize that others might be in the same situation. Recognizing what niche you can fill is crucial to discovering the unique contributions you can make.

Creating a Career Plan: Where to Start?

"When I sit and talk to veterans, I'm inspired by them. It's personal."[2] So says Melvin Kearney, an army veteran turned *Nashville* actor and veterans advocate. Melvin didn't know that supporting veterans would become part of his calling. In fact, his life plan was completely, totally different: His dream was to be a U.S. Marshal. But then he encountered a 19-year-old kid who lost both his legs. "When I looked at him, I kept thinking, 'back in that mission, that could have been me that lost both my legs.' It's not about my plan; it's about God's plan. So I decided, I'm going to try to inspire veterans every day." Being on television gave Melvin a platform to make his voice heard and let soldiers transitioning out of the military know that it's possible to make something big happen with your life. "If you've got that calling and you 'walk the walk,' you're going to be okay," he says.

Career advice used to center on the maxim to "do what you love." But more and more, there's a shift toward the idea that following your bliss is not the best way to go when it comes to your career. First of all, you run the risk of growing weary of a favorite hobby. For example, Ali loves to bake bread to relax, and make cakes and pies for her friends' birthdays, but would not want to be a professional baker. It's perfectly okay to use skills and strengths that you enjoy, but it's okay to keep that as an accent rather than your focus.

How do you find the exact spot where the thing that you love and the thing that other people will care about—and pay for—overlap? If the thing that you're excited to wake up for in the morning is the same thing that makes someone say, "Wow, this is something that is truly worthwhile and helpful to me," then that intersection is where you should be focusing your time and energy.

Once you get psyched up to build your brand, you'll want to make big changes all at once, so it can be hard to hold yourself to taking small, strategic steps. But in order to get to this new place in your life, there are a few vital points you must first consider. Here is our framework:

Building a Compelling Narrative Using RAPTURE

Humans have a natural desire to tell stories to ourselves and to each other. Unless you develop a cohesive narrative, it's easy for your audience to form a haphazard perception of what you're doing. If you're making a big change, you have to find a way to describe that transition to other people. You don't have to seek universal approval, but in order to get job opportunities and client referrals, to be recognized and really embraced in your new role, you need to think about how you're presenting this trajectory to your audience.

All compelling narratives have a few things in common. You want to enchant and delight your audience. In fact, you might just say that you want to leave them in RAPTURE, the acronym we use for thinking about developing compelling narratives:

- 👍 **R**elevant: The story of your brand should center around its most core components, the strongest and most unique features.

- 👍 **A**uthentic: You need to believe in your narrative and come across as genuine. If you're not moved by your brand ideals, how could you expect to move others?

- 👍 **P**ersuasive: Your narrative needs to be compelling enough to draw others in.

- 👍 **T**imely: As your brand develops, so should your narrative. It is not a fixed construct, and needs to evolve as your brand changes shape. You should not be working with a brand statement that's out of date.

- ✤ **U**nderstandable: Be clear and direct. Vague descriptions or convoluted brand statements make a bad first impression. People should not have to work to understand what you're saying; they should recognize your intentions from the get-go.

- ✤ **R**elatable: People trust those with whom they can empathize. They need to be able to imagine themselves in your shoes if your aim is to have them support you.

- ✤ **E**ducational: Your brand statement is, essentially, your elevator pitch. It should say something to your audience about what you do and who you are.

RAPTURE is especially important if you're in the midst of a career transition. You need to control your narrative and be able to explain your transition in a way that makes sense. Why are you going from one thing to another? How does your past experience add value to your new endeavor? The best way to show this progression is by creating content. Whether you like to blog, create videos, or make podcasts—and we'll discuss some of these ways to make your voice heard in the next chapter—doing *something* shows people that you're committed to and aligned with your new trajectory. Depending on the nature of the transition, there may be doubts about your ability to be effective in your new area, so take every opportunity to prove that you're serious and committed to your new direction.

Once you're started down that path, how do you know when your plan is working? There can be lag time between when you start to put yourself out there and when you start to get feedback, and the way that you deal with this gap is incredibly important. As uncomfortable as this time may be, follow the advice of the great Winston Churchill: "When you're going through hell, keep going." (There's some debate if Churchill actually said it, but either way, it's a pretty good rallying cry.) Expect some ups and downs, because bouts of uncertainty are normal during a period of transition. But once you've committed to your new path, it's time to embrace it. The more you immerse yourself in your new identity, the better.

Before Developing Your Personal Brand Statement

It is imperative that you know what your brand is by the time you decide to start engaging with your audience. To start out, we recommend with thinking how you would sum yourself up in three words. "Loud, optimistic, and colorful" is how Bradford Shellhammer describes himself.[3] He's the cofounder and CEO of Bezar, who rose to fame after cofounding Fab, Ali's old employer. There'll be plenty more on Bradford later. Melvin Kearney, the *Nashville* actor, describes himself as "humble, dedicated, and passionate." To Melvin, humility is one of the most important attributes one can embrace and strive for. "I'm nothing without the support of family, friends, and God; that keeps me grounded."

Now, Melvin is an interesting guy. It's not too often that you meet a U.S. military veteran turned actor and veterans' advocate. He's played Bo, the bodyguard of Hayden Panettiere's character, on the ABC drama *Nashville* since 2012. Melvin sees laying out a personal branding statement—and strategy—as an important tool for success. "I want to set an example for others coming after me, anyone who has a hope or dream," Melvin tells us. As a veteran soldier, he chooses his words cautiously, and he selects opportunities that match his personal style and vision.

The initial steps in personal branding involve establishing a general framework for how you define yourself. This includes your voice, your personality, and your approach to interacting with your social audience. These key attributes will be incredibly important as you work to become better known, and will be crucial components of your strategy.

After all, considering the importance of communication, you've got to refine your brand before sharing it with the outside world. Be very clear as you identify your mission and convey your brand's values. What does your brand believe in? What does your brand feel passionately about? What is your brand selling? (We'll answer this one: It's the *value* the customer gets from your product. Make sure that most of your engagement with your customer base can relate back to the value you're creating for them.)

Once you've built up this image and you're sure that your brand has a clear identity, the next step is to improve the odds that your audience will recognize you across all platforms. The simplest way to be cohesive is to choose the same or similar profile pictures, headlines, and descriptive texts for your brand.

Your social voice needs to reflect you—not just your personality, but also your own experiences. If you have a background that sets you apart, make sure that your strategy is built with this distinctive quality in mind.

You have to display value in who you are and what you've accomplished, as that value is generally transferrable to other areas. If you've achieved results in one area, that still matters, even if it isn't directly relevant to a different position. Focus on your accomplishments.

Writing Your Personal Brand Statement

Let's talk about the new you. How are you different from "You 1.0"? And what is it about you that's different from everyone else? If you can successfully position yourself as special and distinct in a professional setting, your narrative should parallel this line of thought. What value do you bring to the table that's unique to you?

As of this moment, you need to think of yourself differently. Forget about thinking of yourself as an employee. You don't belong to any company. You're not defined by your job title or day-to-day responsibilities. You're a brand as much as Coke, Nike, or Cover Girl. Ask yourself the same question that brand managers of companies ask themselves: How is my product or service different?

Defining Your Unique Identity

The initial steps in personal branding involve establishing a general framework for how you define yourself. This includes your voice, your personality, and your approach to interacting with your social audience. These key attributes will be incredibly important as you work to become known digitally, and the way in which you engage people will determine your brand's social strategy.

Identify the qualities or characteristics that make you stand out from your competitors. If you're going to be a brand, you have to be relentless. Try comparing yourself to another brand, maybe somebody who does something similar, whether it's a coworker or another team that works in a related sphere.

Ask yourself:

- 👍 What do I do that adds remarkable, measurable, distinctive value?
- 👍 What have I done as recently as this week to make myself distinct?
- 👍 What have I accomplished that I can unabashedly be proud of?
- 👍 What would my colleagues and customers say is my greatest strength?
- 👍 What is my most noteworthy personal trait?
- 👍 Ultimately, what do I want to be known for?

Write down your answers. Then, condense your response to fewer than 15 words. Take the time to look this over and refine it. If your answer to this question wouldn't light up the eyes of your prospective audience—or if it doesn't even grab you—then it's time to put thought and effort into reimagining and redeveloping your brand statement.

Some additional things to consider at this point in the process include: What's your brand's future benefit model? Do you deliver your work on time every time, giving dependable, reliable service to your customers? Do you anticipate and solve problems before they've become a crisis so your client saves money and anguish just by having you on the team? Do you always complete your projects within budget?

Next, what do you want to be known for and how do you want to position it? No matter what your skill set is, no matter what your future benefit is, you still have to have incredible marketing so that your customers, your colleagues, and your network all think of you first and foremost.

Let's add some context here. You grew your department by 12 percent in the last quarter. Is that good or bad? If all the other departments shrank, or if you grew your department while cutting costs, that's much more relevant than just a figure by itself.

From here, you can start to develop your pitch. Think of a screenplay. Even though your life contains thousands of events and plots, it makes sense to distill the narrative to a handful of compelling and relevant themes. This is exactly what you have to do in order to create a powerful personal brand.

Think of the short-term version of your pitch as a book-jacket blurb. A few short, punchy phrases that grab your potential reader's attention and make them want to learn more. The long-term version of your pitch is more like a career retrospective speech. Imagine you're getting a lifetime achievement award. What would you want your acceptance speech—or the toasts in your honor—to say?

Once you have answered these questions, you will not only have a foundation on which to build your voice, but you will be more confident in your brand when networking with peers or speaking to your audience. This will also help you find out if your brand has any weaknesses that need to be addressed.

When writing your personal brand statement, make sure you're as tightly focused and specific as possible. We all know we need to be focusing on our careers and how we present ourselves, right? Yet there are plenty of professionals out there who don't focus. Many professionals have an unfocused, scattered approach as a result of insecurity, because the job market is so tough and competitive. They think that they should be generalists and cast a wider net, but the opposite is true: Specificity can make you the best fit for the job rather than one of many also-rans.

When Adam Cohen first started looking for blog advice, he turned to the numerous "mom blogs" that were available, but they didn't quite match up with his needs. "There were a couple of dad blogs," he tells us, "but they were all very California-based. I'm a New Yorker by heart, so that kind of peace-loving, hippie kind of stuff didn't really work for me. And on the flipside, there were dads who were almost bitter about fatherhood, and that wasn't the experience I was having either." By studying the market, Adam identified an opportunity for a caring, but practical source of advice from a dad's perspective.

Giving Your Brand a Voice

In order to make sure your content stands out from the crowd, your social voice needs to be well defined. The ability to describe your brand voice in a concise manner can pay huge dividends for your personal brand, because you can revisit your original blueprints and see if the way you're speaking is truly the way you wish to be perceived.

The way you sound when speaking to people across digital channels should resonate with them and be as unique as your own fingerprints. Just as Adam did, you have to find your tone. This process begins with an examination of the strengths and qualities your brand has to offer, which will influence how you present yourself. Figure out what you have to offer that others do not, and build your voice around that unique trait.

Consistency is key: Success comes from a recognizable voice across all channels, from Facebook to Twitter to e-mail to conversations occurring at conferences. The easiest way to remain consistent is to remain authentic. In addition to knowing what you are, you have to know what you are not. Adopt a voice that reflects your brand's values and attributes rather than someone else's, and it will not only ring true, but also save you the hassle of having to meticulously craft your voice to suit some manufactured standard.

Having an *identifiable* social voice is just as important, if not more, as having a *unique* social voice. Subtle nuances in tone, attitude, and disposition all come across in a social voice. Those elements, together with all the brand cues surrounding the brand—typeface, color palette, shapes, and logo—work to create a personality.

Keep in mind that something might work in a face-to-face conversation, but not nearly as well for social media. That's what our friend Melvin Kearney from *Nashville* discovered. As he says, "At one point in my life I was very sarcastic, but I realized I can't be so sarcastic on social media because what I might think is funny, or my buddies might think is funny, someone might take the wrong way, and all of a sudden you're in a social media nightmare, and you're in the news the next day. It comes with great responsibility."

Once you've made the proper adjustments, if your social voice is identifiable, you'll attract the right people, who have the potential to become your Most Valuable Customers (MVCs). They will be more likely to share your brand's values, tastes, and preferences—and even share your content with their networks. Communicating with an identifiable voice helps strike up engagement with the "right" target audience.

When it's Time to Pivot

In basketball, a pivot is a movement in which the player holding the ball may move in any direction to avoid obstacles by driving their "pivot" foot off the floor. In business, a pivot is much the same thing: It builds upon the position where you are right now, yet allows you to change direction in some way and move past blocks or stalls. In basketball, a pivot is all about seeing an opportunity in a different direction from the way you are currently going, and changing course.

That's the same principle regarding a pivot in business. When you're in the process of pivoting, or rebranding, you must find the through line—a connecting theme or plot in a story—that connects what you were just doing to what you are about to do. Ideally, the story of how you started at point A and arrived at point B will portray you as strategic and focused, and not like someone who wanders through life like a tourist in Times Square. Tell a story that excites and impresses people. We're not expecting it to be as exciting as *Captain America: Civil War*, but it has to be the best possible, most authentic version of your story it can be.

General Communication Skills

It's important to fine-tune your story so that it will be clear to your audience. People are busy and have short attention spans, so make sure that the traits your narrative conveys aren't generic. Many professionals want to be known for their leadership. However, there are plenty of people who can lay claim to this attribute. Be as specific as possible. "Good at contract negotiation" says much more about your unique skill set. If you're "a quick learner with new database technologies," say so! It's important to look at your entire career for traits and themes that are less general, and more specific to you. This isn't easy, but it's well worth the effort. Tell a relevant story that is different from what prospective employers, partners, and clients typically hear, and you will stand head and shoulders above your competition.

Jeremy has pivoted multiple times throughout his career. After starting out as a graphic designer and Webmaster right after college, he built upon this skill set to become a Web developer, which gave him the tools to start his own business. That new acumen helped him get into business school and earn his MBA. Jeremy then used that degree, along with his previous Web development experience, to become the marketing manager running e-commerce departments for a number of beauty brands at conglomerates such as L'Oreal and Unilever. He then built upon his e-commerce experience to focus on social media within the beauty sector. Later, he used this social media experience to write *Going Social*, a book on how to build strong digital brands. Afterward, he wrote a book (spoiler alert: You're looking at it), which is still about brands and social media, but focuses on *personal* brands and social media, with plenty of non-digital best practices as well. Jeremy has moved pretty far away from graphic design, but when you look at each individual step, his path makes complete sense.

In hindsight, all of these steps through the course of Jeremy's career may seem like the obvious decisions. At the time, they were not guaranteed to be successful. But they all had one thing in common: They pivoted off of previous successes in order to create new opportunities.

In basketball, a pivot is completely allowed and necessary. If you pivot without picking up the other foot, you aren't called for traveling, and you aren't forced to relinquish the ball to the other team. But perceptions matter. If the referee doesn't notice that you had a foot firmly planted on the ground, you might get called for traveling. So it's not just about what you do—it's about what other people think you've done. The same principle applies with respect to your personal branding. You might think you have had a successful pivot from one part of your career to another, but this transition has to be clear to others. If the transition is not clear to other people, it doesn't exist.

Of course, not everybody has a pivot in their career: sometimes somebody has a moment where their life gets changed in an instant. That's what happened to Ali when her husband graduated from medical school and matched at a residency in Philadelphia. Although Pennsylvania is hardly the ends of the earth, it still represented a change for the two lifelong New Yorkers. It was one thing for Ali to accept that she would move for her husband's new job. It was another to acclimate to a new city and try to reestablish herself without her usual network. Ali reached out to numerous colleagues, clients, and former coworkers to try to build a new community of contacts, make connections, and find opportunities in her new home. Ali has now been in Philadelphia for two years. She'll always be a New Yorker at heart, but she's worked hard to make the most of her new situation.

If you're like Ali and a key moment changed the trajectory of both your life and your professional career, you need to embrace it and lean into it. It's part of your narrative. Turn the page and we'll show you how to express that narrative to your audience.

Chapter 3

Ways to Make Your Voice Heard via Content

Why Create Content?

Creating more opportunities to reach others leads to good things. A large volume of positive, high-quality content enhances your business success because it makes you more visible to prospects. You never know where clients or recruiters are looking; you might be found in a YouTube tutorial, a guest article written on a well-regarded industry blog, a link to your podcast, some video of you speaking at a conference, and more.

This is how Jeremy ended up getting a major client for his branding firm Firebrand Group. After the editor in chief of *Consumer Reports* read *Going Social*, she reached out to Jeremy. Ultimately, *Consumer Reports* hired Firebrand to work on a key project—and the visibility from that partnership then led to work with other prominent clients.

The more content you create, the more you can get in front of the people you want to reach. This is also why we recommend creating accounts on more than one platform. You might feel more comfortable on Twitter than Facebook (or vice versa), but you want to get in front of as many eyes as possible. Most platforms make it simple to cross-post and cross-promote, so don't ever feel like you have to be monogamous in this respect. Google and other search engines look for relevant content because it's good business for them. We'll explore these topics more in future chapters.

Getting an attractive headshot helps, too, as that will often be the first thing people see about you.

Not all of your activity has to be directly related to your work, but it should still have a purpose. For instance, an entertainer could intersperse some clever and funny tweets along with updates about new or upcoming projects. Find a good, engaging way to get your message through to your audience, and do it in such a way that people will remember who you are as well as what you're saying.

Serving up a Slice

"I spend a lot of time doing *What's Gaby Cooking*—I basically live and breathe it. That doesn't bother me, because I love my brand and I love what I do."[1]

This philosophy is what gives Gaby Dalkin—the entrepreneur behind the popular food blog *What's Gaby Cooking*—the energy and enthusiasm to hammer out content. Gaby is squarely in the digital media food world, which entails many hats rolled up into one: She's also a food writer, food host, cookbook author, and more. It's hard to put a label on what she does, because there are so many different sides to her business; New Media Food Influencer seems to wrap it up into one neat little sound bite.

After college, Gaby moved to Los Angeles and, with little previous food experience, went to culinary school and started a blog. "I had no idea it would actually turn into something that was lucrative," she admits. But as the site started to get popular and picked up speed, she realized that not only was building her brand a lot of fun, but she could make it profitable if she focused on it from a business perspective.

Gaby is one of the many people who have found that becoming an author and content creator helps you become an authority. Tailor your medium to fit your message and your audience. If you specialize in giving advice to clients, you may want to focus on building a series of videos addressing frequently asked questions. The more you present your expertise in a way that others want to absorb and engage with, the more you'll represent the personal brand you're looking to be known for.

Everyone wants to stand out, and sometimes it's tempting to raise your voice and "shout" to be heard over all the noise. But lowering your voice in a crowded room makes people lean closer to hear what you have to say. You don't need to be louder than everyone else; if you have something worthwhile to share, people will listen.

Text is an important medium, so it's worth putting some work into developing your writing. From blogging on your own Website to writing articles for others, there are many different writing formats and venues to consider. But if writing isn't your jam, don't worry—your content creation doesn't have to take that form. Here are some other ways in which you can make your voice heard:

- Photos: It's easy to share pictures of your daily life, from snapshots of food and friends to the ubiquitous (and infamous) #selfie. But ask yourself: How can you add your unique spin to this medium? How can you tie your pictures back to your brand?

- Videos: Movies are dynamic and attention grabbing, but can take some skill to do well. Is the work you do a good fit for this format?

- Podcasts: If you're more comfortable speaking than writing, creating an audio series can be a great option for engaging with your audience.

✍ Presentations: Websites such as SlideShare are great for sharing your work if you think in slides, especially if you're in the B2B world.

All of this takes time. Not just a little bit of time, but a significant amount. This includes a big chunk of prep in the beginning and continuous maintenance through time. You have to put in the effort to create, and promote, and repeat, even when the return on investment isn't immediate. That's not to say the investment isn't worth it; getting heard is a major plus in building your personal brand. But patience is definitely required.

No matter what format(s) you choose, though, this chapter will show you how to select the right strategy, platforms, and tools to show off your brand in the best light.

Ways to Get Out There

So how do you make your voice heard? There are no limits to the ways you can go about enhancing your image. You could try moonlighting and working for another project inside an existing organization that you belong to, or freelancing on a project that introduces you to a totally new group of people. If you do good work for them, they'll probably do some of the promoting work for you. You could also try teaching a class at a community college or in an adult educational program at your own company if they do skill sharing.

When people see you as an expert, it increases your standing as a professional. That makes it more likely that people will come to you with requests and opportunities for you to stand out from the crowd. You could also try writing a column or an opinion piece for your favorite publication. Think of a Website that you like and think of something that you could contribute. Maybe not a site as well known as *Mashable* or *The Huffington Post*, at first, but you can start off with smaller publications and then use those clips to leverage for more openings.

Customers as Content

Now, some people think of content very narrowly, and immediately start thinking of books and articles alone. But, as noted content expert Ann Handley points out, so much of what you produce is, in fact, content. The product pages on your Website? Content. The slider of images on your homepage? Content. The copy that leads in to the contact form on your Website? You get the picture.

To that point, one great form of content is customer testimonials. Now, by customers, we really mean constituents: former bosses and coworkers, clients, peers, and so on. A great way to convey what your brand stands for is to let your fans do the talking via written and video testimonials. We recommend giving your customers very basic guidelines on what you're looking for, including attributes you are looking to emphasize—but let them know you want completely honest feedback. If your audience sees that customers are giving uncensored points of view, it will help to establish trust.

The more "raw" a customer testimonial is, the more authentic it feels. A hand-written note scanned as an image and posted on your Website has a more human quality than a highly produced customer video, despite the fact that the former is far cheaper. Just think about it: Why would you spend more to create a polished piece of content if it's less likely to accomplish your objectives?

The Trick Successful People Use to Create Great Content

One of the most famous pieces of writing advice is "write drunk, edit sober." Writers often quote the adage, encouraging others to do what is necessary to overcome writer's block, self-doubt, and creative lapses. But this strategy is perfect for content developers of all kinds, including entrepreneurs, graphic designers, videographers, and more.

Don't take this advice too literally, of course. Anyone who has tried to do creative work while truly drunk can tell you that you are more likely to pass out at your desk with a movie playing and half a slice of pizza stuck to your forehead than you are to produce any sort of real work. Writing drunk, creating drunk—they're about losing yourself in the work: submitting yourself to momentum, getting swept up in creative bursts, and immersing yourself so deeply that you're almost giddy with possibility.

Bringing this approach to content development can be just as effective. Getting *that* into your output will allow you to develop the most passionate, genuine message. Taking risks, allowing excitement to get the best of you, sharing too much—people struggle with these liberations out of fear of overexposure. Here are a few ways we advise you make the most of "planning drunk":

- **Take risks.** It's possible that your current methods already work; they get the job done, but they don't really make a huge impact. But odds are you didn't get into this business in order to play it safe all the time; you did it to find interest and excitement. Sometimes the biggest risk is not taking one at all.

- **Don't be afraid to look stupid.** This is something drunk people do exceptionally well, and it's a perspective you should embrace in your approach to strategy. There are thousands of good ideas that have gone unexplored because of people's unwillingness to look like an idiot. No one remembers the real duffers that fall to the floor, but that one-in-a-million, crazy idea from left field might just be a knockout.

- **Don't be afraid to show emotion or to show your audience some love.** You don't have to be that guy who goes around at 1 a.m. trying to kiss everybody, but if you show your audience you care, they will return that affection with enthusiasm.

- **Have fun.** The best kind of drunk and the best kind of brand strategy, being fun is a surefire way to make a big impact. This is especially true on social media, an arena in which content is often stale, and where people can sometimes be very unpleasant. People respond well to happiness, and playful content can have very positive results.

It's easy to overlook the "sober" half of the process; after all, the drunkenness is the fun part, right? Not necessarily. The drunken planning may be more exciting, but assessing and implementing those ideas can be just as satisfying, if not more so. Here's how to get the most out of your drunken idea generation:

- 👍 **Clean up.** Once you've amassed a series of creative, crazy ideas, go through them and deliberate over which ones could be actionable. As you sober up, you may find your cautiousness returning in full force. Don't be too hasty to dismiss ideas until you're absolutely sure they're not usable.

- 👍 **Get some rest.** Give your ideas time to percolate. As with writing, a small buffer period lets you look at your work with fresh eyes. Let the partially formed ideas stew a little, reducing in your mind until you're left with a more cohesive, more condensed result.

- 👍 **Follow up.** You'd call that cute girl or guy you met last night, right? Don't let that sort of opportunity slip away with your newly discovered content plan, either. Get the ball rolling on your actionable ideas, and move on anything that needs to be implemented right away.

But wait, there's an Act III. What, you think we'd forget about the hangover? Don't worry, you won't need Advil and a bagel sandwich for this one.

Once you've picked out the viable ideas from planning drunk and published the polished results, there are still going to be little bits and pieces lying around: extras that might have been good ideas but didn't quite fit, or lines of thought that you didn't stop to explore in the heat of the moment. Think of those as the flask in the couch cushions or the half case of beer behind the fridge. Remember where you're hiding those—they may just be the fuel for your next award-winning piece of content.

Getting Others to Promote You

If you're reluctant to promote yourself, or feel that you might come across as a showoff, collaborating with a friend or colleague can be valuable. We don't mean someone who promotes you for no reason—what would be the point? Think of it in terms of the more traditional job hunt. If a good friend works for a company you're interested in, would you apply blindly through their Website, or would you ask them to pass along your resume to the hiring manager? Your connections and network will raise your profile much higher than you can all by yourself.

Creating—and Curating—Engaging Images and Photographs

Gaby Dalkin of *What's Gaby Cooking* is a big fan of using social media to drive her brand. Her favorite social platform is Instagram, though she loves Pinterest as well. "My brand is such a visual one," she says. "I can write 140 characters and put it out on Twitter, but unless there's a picture with it, it's not going to get the response it would on Pinterest or Instagram."

For Melvin Kearney, the war veteran turned actor we met earlier, it's all about the photos. "They give more life to the story," he explains.[2] At the end of the day, his stories aren't just about himself; they're about the people who have supported him and touched his life in a compelling way. Photos—and videos—are crucial in that regard. "I want you to see my photos and see where I came from. Because facts and figures are forgotten; stories are remembered and retold forever." Melvin wants his audience to see his photos and be inspired. "I want you to look at my photos and see: Okay, this guy's from a small town. He's in the military. Huh. I could do it too; it's possible. This guy's on television, because he took a chance. He showed up, he stayed positive. I can do that. That can be me."

We've already established the importance of image sharing in branding, so it's a good idea to develop a strategy related to photographs and other static visual content on social channels like Instagram.

Another highly visual platform to take notice of is Pinterest. Like many similar social services, Pinterest has a pin-it bookmarklet that users can add to their browser toolbars, making pinning images (and making them social) incredibly easy for many users. Though a lot of early users focused their pins on arts and crafts, there's no right or wrong way to use Pinterest. As more users sign up, the type of content being pinned becomes increasingly diverse.

When images are pinned to Pinterest, they are automatically linked back to their original source, so Pinterest is capable of driving considerable referral traffic to your Website. In fact, by some accounts, it drives more traffic than Google+, YouTube, and LinkedIn combined.[3]

All of this interaction makes it relatively easy to make connections with Pinterest users who may be interested in your products or services. Think about the kinds of things that will help your audience before you think about what you want from them, and you'll have a chance of winning their loyalty.

Creating Engaging Video Content

Producing online video content can be an extremely useful branding tool and an effective way to engage more deeply with your existing audience. After all, it gives your brand a human face, and makes you more relatable.

Videos can also help you reach new audiences and build buzz around your brand—take Mike Polk, for example. The Cleveland-area comedian launched the comically critical "Hastily Made Cleveland Tourism Video" on YouTube in April 2009, and bolstered his career with a single stroke. You shouldn't expect a single video to make or break your brand, but you can see just how powerful video can be.

Although still photography is key to her brand, Gaby Dalkin leverages video when she feels incredibly strongly about a particular dish or ingredient. "I want people to see my excitement firsthand, and see how pumped I am about the recipes," Gaby says. She also realizes that video is increasingly becoming a huge tool for food marketers: Their audiences want to see food and the preparation process on video. "I won't post something if it's not pretty," she says. "I know that people want to see something beautiful that inspires them to get in the kitchen."

And, once again, the importance of search engine optimization comes up. Creating a popular stream of videos will make your brand more likely to pop up on Google. Multiply the effects of videos by sharing them on your other social channels as well. If you put out several unique messages, you can test to see which gain the most traction. Just make sure your video is high quality. Today, video quality is not just an advantage—it's a requirement. What's acceptable varies depending on your sector; aim to be in the 75th percentile or above of your direct competitors. If you want your content to resonate, a good camera and a knack for editing are essential. Let your audience know that you truly care, and respect how much their time is worth. If you don't take your video efforts seriously, no one else will, either.

But production is just the first step; a huge part of the process is digital strategy and seeding to promote the video launch. Distribution and promotion strategy is something you have to keep in mind before you ever start rolling.

Though you shouldn't go *too* out there when creating digital content, it can help to step away from traditional advertising formulas and create content that gives more to the audience than promotion. This kind of value can come in the form of information, entertainment, inspiration, or a combination of the above.

Many people dream of their video going viral, but that should never be the goal. In fact, by having that goal in mind, you're less likely to actually go viral, and more likely to embarrass yourself in the process. Just focus on developing a compelling video with your target audience in mind. And, like with all social media efforts, don't expect too much from each individual video. It's the cumulative effect that matters.

You may find yourself stuck in a market that's flooded with competitors, and it can feel impossible to cut through the white noise, but there are ways around that if you carefully map out your strategy. There are certain key points to hit, and common pitfalls to avoid. About 95 percent of your competition will fall prey to these, so if you can follow some basic principles, you will put yourself in a position to stand out in a positive way.

There is still a lot of room for growth and development of video as a marketing tool, but there are already many examples of brands that have successfully used video to improve engagement. As we'll see next, YouTube channels are a perfect example of this phenomenon.

However, make sure you pay attention to one preliminary step that people so often skip: Do your homework. If you have no idea what's successful, how will you know what to do? Take advantage of the research others have done for you: identify their mistakes so you can avoid doing the same, watch for emerging trends, and analyze the common factors in popular channels.

Solid Content

One strong example (no pun intended) is fitness channels on YouTube. With such a broad and ubiquitous platform as YouTube, everything from music to makeup tutorials to gaming to competitive eating are packed with hopefuls. The audience is diverse, fickle, and has a very short attention span. How do you win people over and keep them in the fold? Let's assume you're starting a YouTube channel. For argument's sake, we'll talk about fitness channels, though the following lessons can be applied to whatever type of personal endeavor you'd like to spotlight on YouTube—beauty, unboxing, sports commentary, you name it.

Sometimes it seems like half of the people who've ever wandered into a gym think it's a good idea to start up a channel, making it very difficult for newer YouTube channels to prove themselves. So, where should you start?

Be likeable and relatable. The YouTubers who have found success—Christian Guzman,[4] Maxx Chewning,[5] and the like—are entertaining. On a more fundamental level, though, their audiences tune in because these stars are also nice guys who generate interest in their lives. Maxx has done more than 70 "IIFYM Full Day of Eating" (If It Fits Your Macros, a flexible dieting method) videos, in which the camera follows him around all day. These 15-plus-minute videos don't provide revolutionary information or great recipes; the guy eats cereal half the time and talks about his travel bag pretty darn often. But the genuine approach and this sort of friend-by-proxy relationship draws viewers in. Like a television show, we're fascinated by these characters and become emotionally invested.

Figure out your actual brand and market yourself. Don't market your personality traits or the intangibles, but your actual brand. All of these YouTube channels have clothing lines, which allow them to both monetize the channels even further than Google AdSense, and for them to involve their fanbase beyond views. With a couple of words—Christian Guzman's Alphalete Athletics, for example—you turn your fans into your "team," and make them feel like participants in your life. This is a huge win for the brand. When a person buys your shirt and wears it to the gym, they feel as though they're representing you, and they're reinforcing that connection in their own mind in addition to advertising for you.

Like other ultra-competitive fields, fitness and bodybuilding stars are separated by marketing and a little bit of luck. If you're making a channel, it's about much more than just how you look, or how much you can lift. Some of the key characteristics that set these channels apart are:

1. **Production value.**

   Watching these channels can seem like a cross between fitness and an introduction to cinematography. As channels progress, their cameras improve from iPhone camera to point-and-shoot to DSLR to nicer DSLR, until they're spending upward of a few thousand dollars on cameras and microphones. You don't exactly have to invest in a production company from day one, but make sure you have good lighting, decent video, smooth editing, and quality audio. This last piece is one of the most commonly overlooked aspects, yet can be an absolute deal-breaker for your YouTube channel. Nobody wants to listen to a bunch of static or hear you trying to shout over the air conditioner.

2. **Consistency.**

Your audience won't patiently stick around if you're putting out one video every two weeks; people stay with channels because the videos become part of their daily routine. Maybe they watch your videos before they go to the gym or when they're eating breakfast. Having a reliable source of entertainment or motivation is crucial to attracting a loyal audience.

3. **Niche.**

What kind of YouTuber are you? Do you put together video compilations set to epic music? Are you a scientist who's focused on programming and the biology/physiology side of things? Carving out a space for yourself will bring in the kind of viewers you want; once you have an established base, you're freer to appeal to a wider audience.

4. **Social media.**

Apart from YouTube, it's critical to engage in other platforms, especially those with a visual aspect. Obviously, bodybuilding and powerlifting are things people want to see more than they want to hear about, so Instagram and Vine are particularly useful. Meals, progress pictures, personal records—these are great things to share with your audience. Once you really find and develop your voice, having a Twitter base will also contribute a good deal to your presence.

As with any endeavor requiring a strong brand, YouTubers also know how to recover from mistakes. Sometimes, debates or contention between YouTubers can land them in hot water when they say something rash or unintentionally offensive. With such an active community, word travels fast. A YouTuber can go to bed content and blissfully unaware that when she wakes up in the morning, she may find a very angry response from viewers.

There are a plethora of intangibles to success as a YouTuber, but hitting these main points and staying determined are absolutely crucial if you want to give yourself a chance at success. The field is constantly evolving, so if you keep your ear to the ground about new or upcoming trends and can get on top of changes before anyone else, you will gain yourself a following in a community that is always hungry for knowledge and new developments.

Once you have a good grasp of the audience, the first consideration is the simplest, though not necessarily the easiest: Put out quality content. If you don't believe in what you're putting out there, how will anyone else? If this is the case, you may want to reevaluate your plan and wait until you're more prepared. Having solid content will put you above most people, but no one is going to listen to a skinny guy struggling to do a pushup—unless that's both your angle and your target audience.

Engage in the Community

There is significant horizontal movement among viewers. Though members of any given YouTuber's audience pick favorites, they typically will not limit themselves to a single channel. Information is secondary to entertainment in this medium, and there is much more room to provide the latter. If you can provide humor or information, then people will not only check you out, they'll stay with you. You're not necessarily in direct competition with your fellow YouTubers, and can take advantage of their fanbase if you get to know the people behind the channels. Reaching out, asking for advice, or even participating in comments can get you noticed.

Social media is social. It's even in the name. You're not yelling into a vacuum, and you can't treat it like a broadcast medium. You have an audience, and there's got to be give and take between you and the people consuming what you produce.

A perfect example of this relationship is *EpicMealTime*, a YouTube cooking show in which the creators cook up monstrosities of meals, racking up the calorie counts with huge amounts of bacon, meat, and booze. The amped-up, foul-mouthed Quebec natives up the ante with every video, displaying calorie counts over 100,000 on screen to boast of their culinary overkill. The show's been around since 2010, so you'd think the shtick would be pretty stale, but *EpicMealTime* keeps it fresh by using and responding to audience feedback.

But the show doesn't go for your typical audience dialogue. *EpicMealTime's* brand is ironic and farcical, and the hosts take the same tone with their views: teasing them, taunting them, and even jokingly calling them out. The main host and voiceover, Harley, addresses the imaginary "haters" that allegedly trash-talk the show.

For all its mock assaults on its audience, though, *EpicMealTime* is buoyed by a very strong social media presence. The hosts promote their Instagram and Twitter accounts heavily, encouraging conversation. From tongue-in-cheek retaliatory insults to requests for future meals, the audience engages with the creators of the show, providing an almost endless source of material for future episodes. It's a brilliant strategy. *EpicMealTime* both crowdsources its material while connecting with its fans. The give and take nature of the ribbing between the show and its fans is similar to the sort of relationships men of that age and background have with their friends, which helps the audience feel a bond with the show's characters.

Branding Yourself Through Writing

The Perfect Blog Post in 9 Steps

Whether it's for *Inc.*, the Firebrand Group Insights section, or elsewhere, Jeremy is constantly writing. And if you have a blog, you probably want to increase traffic and maximize engagement with your audience, too. The best way to do that is to not only share ridiculously captivating content, but also present it in the ideal way. It's not as tricky as it sounds. Here's our nine-step checklist to strive for blog perfection:

1. **Craft a short, snappy headline.**

   Headlines are read more than any other text on a Website. You could have the most fascinating article in the history of the Internet, but if you don't have an eye-catching headline, the reader will just keep scrolling or click away. Get your point across in a clear, direct way. Be concise: Statistics suggest that readers tend to absorb *the first and last three words of a headline.*

2. **Use an opening hook.**

   A great headline will grab the reader's attention. A strong intro will keep it. If you can catch someone's interest in the first three or four sentences, that person is more likely to read the entire article. Research[6] by Buffer finds that the best way to introduce a new post is through storytelling; in fact, sharing a compelling narrative can attract 300 percent more readers. If you're unsure how to begin a post, lead with a personal anecdote.

3. **Include photos and other visuals.**

   Forty percent of readers will respond better to visual information than plain text.[7] We're naturally drawn to visual content, and photos and graphics are an essential component of social media marketing and user experience. Though a well-written post is important, images have a quick and powerful impact, and are easy to digest and share.

4. **Limit the number of characters per line.**

   Help your readers process text, especially key segments of your piece. The best way to do this—without skimping on content—is to place an image next to a particularly important phrase. Don't be afraid to play around with formatting; boost the font size of your opening paragraph and see how it looks.

5. **Incorporate subheadings for better readability.**

We've all heard about our society's ever-shrinking attention span. It happens all too often that a reader's mind starts to wander halfway through a post. But if someone sees an interesting subhead farther down the page, it will likely prompt them to continue.

From a reader's perspective, subheads make the material easier to absorb and helps them scan and skip to the sections they find most appealing.

6. **Keep the length close to 1,200 words.**

After analyzing 100 top-ranking blog posts, Blog Pros[8] found that long copy outperforms short copy, with an ideal length of 1,149 words per article. "As we strive for leanness, we shouldn't sacrifice the inclusion of data or links to our sources," says Glen Gilmore, noted social media expert and principal of the Gilmore Business Network. Longer articles are usually well researched and have a lot of supporting data, which is why they're shared more frequently.

7. **End with a call to action.**

Ask yourself, "What's the takeaway for the reader?" If you can answer that, you've done your job. "Encourage sharing through strong visuals, snappy data points, and a clear call to action that includes your company handles and any relevant hashtags," says Dina Fierro, the blogger behind the well-known *Eye4Style* fashion and style blog.[9]

8. **Edit, edit, and edit again.**

After your post is complete, read it again—slowly—and have someone you trust read it as well. Even after you publish the piece, read it again and fix small typos that have invariably sneaked past you. "Have you ever thought about sharing an article, but it had a few key typos, so you felt embarrassed?" asks Amy Vernon, prize-winning writer and journalist. "Don't give people any extra reason not to share your posts."[10]

One technique we use to review our writing is the Text-to-Speech option, which is available in most word processing programs and operating systems. Even though it will be read to you in a slightly robotic voice, it forces you to listen to how your blog post flows, and makes it harder for errors to slip past. Ali prefers to check each final draft at least three times: forward, forward out loud, and then each sentence in reverse.

9. **Brevity is the soul of wit.**

   Your time is valuable. So is your audience's. They're not going to trawl through overly dense or rambling paragraphs in order to get the information they want, so condense your post to the most essential information. 1,200 words might be the Platonic ideal, but it's better to have 900 crucial, interesting words than an overblown and under-edited article.

How many of these steps do you prescribe to already? Probably a few, but we're willing to wager that at least a couple of the above represent opportunities for improvement. Make a point of adopting these steps through the next two months and see if it makes a difference.

Blogging on Your Own Site

There are a number of benefits to writing on your own site, including control of the message and the point at which you're hitting your audience from a conversion standpoint. Let us explain.

When you're blogging on a site that you manage yourself, you have a very cooperative editor: yourself. This means that you have full control over when your posts go live, so that you can put them up when you know your target audience is going to be listening, not when an editor decides to fit you in. You also don't run the risk of your message being diluted from an overzealous editor who makes a few well-intentioned edits that, unfortunately, take your article entirely off-course.

The other benefit to writing on your own site is you're hitting your audience near a conversion point. Depending on your line of work, you may define a conversion in a number of ways. It might be filling out a contact form. Or, if you're selling a tangible good, it might be getting your audience members to actually check out on your Website. When you're writing on your own Website, as opposed to someone else's, you're closer in the process of getting someone to convert. This lets you take a different approach to your writing, knowing that you're "near the finish line."

Of course, writing on your own site isn't perfect. Chances are, your on-site audience isn't that robust—at least to begin with. That's why it pays to have a diversified approach and to write elsewhere as well.

Writing Articles for Others

Writing articles for places other than your own Website is a great way to build your brand and gain the awareness you're looking for. Jeremy writes for publications such as *Mashable*, *The Next Web*, and *Inc.* Ali writes for heavily trafficked sites like *BuzzFeed*, *Dwell*, ALOHA, and Birchbox. Publishing content on sites like these gives us exposure to people who likely wouldn't have heard about us otherwise.

It's not just about who initially discovers you, however; equally important is what happens afterward. For example, some of Jeremy's articles on *Inc.* routinely get shared 1,800 times within a week. That's a big deal, because at that point it's not Jeremy branding himself; each member of the audience is marketing Jeremy to his or her own network. They're putting their own brand equity on the line by saying, "Hey, I read this, and I think there's a decent chance you'll find it of value as well."

Of course, when you write for other sites, think of what you want the end result to be. Do you want people to learn more about your company? If so, make sure to link back to your Website in a way that feels organic. Are you looking to get more people to check out your LinkedIn profile? Linking back to specific experiences within your LinkedIn profile will help in that regard. Don't just write to write. Think about how it will help others, which will in turn help you to build and establish your brand.

Branding Yourself Through Audio and E-books

Personal branding in music is more important than ever, especially with the increase in downloads, streaming, and file sharing. Instead of depending on the arm-twisting deals of record companies, artists such as Macklemore can achieve a large following by establishing their brand online.

Authors have similarly expanded options, as the e-book market grows and self-publishing becomes a viable and even preferred method of sharing work. Although traditional publishing is far from dead, the market has certainly changed. Authors such as Deepak Chopra, Gertrude Stein, and Upton Sinclair have self-published works, and there are plenty of advantages to self-publishing. But there's a downside as well: Self-published authors don't get the marketing materials provided by the Big Six, and have to work very hard in order to rise through the ranks, establish their personal brand, and attract the necessary readership to succeed. If you're not Deepak Chopra—if you are, we're huge fans, thanks for reading!—personal branding and establishing a strong digital and offline footprint are going to be key to actually selling some books.

Podcasts

If you're like us, you may have noticed an interesting phenomenon in the last six months: More and more of your colleagues have mentioned a business-centric podcast that you ought to check out, or you've overheard others talking about something they learned from a podcast. Is this the start of a huge new craze?

"Unfortunately the current wave of podcasting is more hype than buzz," says John J. Wall, cohost of *Marketing Over Coffee*, one of the longest-running and most successful marketing podcasts.[11] "I predict a crash in the number of new shows in about six months. As it always does, it will switch from 'We're doing a podcast!' to 'Yeah, podcasting didn't work for us' after one quarter."

We see a spike in new podcasts every now and then in part because entrepreneurs and small businesses want to market themselves and they see audio podcasting as an inexpensive, easy-to-learn cousin of video production. The speed of podcasting works for shows such as *Marketing Over Coffee*, as Wall is acutely aware: "We cover the intersection of marketing and technology, so it's an easy way to get information out there quickly." Though speed to market is an advantage that podcasts possess, production quality still matters. Like most content, if you don't produce great stuff, people will tune you out.

But Wall isn't down on the future of business podcasting at all. "The reality is that there has been steady organic growth for the past eight years," he says. "And that won't change. In spite of the press possibly turning against podcasting [once the current hype cycle is over], it will continue its steady growth."

Despite that likely progression, slow and steady growth hasn't left podcasting with a dominant market share—or, more specifically, ear-share. Edison Research's *Share of Ear* 2014 report found that Americans spent more than four hours a day consuming audio, but only 1.7 percent of that time was spent listening to podcasts. That's certainly not a massive number, considering podcasting has been around since 2004.

Then again, perhaps it's the very fact that podcasting isn't as dominant a media type that makes it so popular with its biggest advocates. "Early adopters have a huge advantage with new marketing techniques. At *Marketing Over Coffee*, we are sharing inside tips with our friends. We really don't want them to spread quickly via every channel, as that would burn our advantage too quickly," says Wall.

Although there are plenty of unknowns about the shape and form of podcasting's growth, Wall is optimistic that podcast lovers have plenty to look forward to: "The people that realize that they can stake out a unique niche will be successful. Podcasting will continue to grow because people love listening to topics they are passionate about, and they can more easily find and consume that content than ever before."

There's no question that there's high quality content out there for consumption. Besides Wall and Christopher S. Penn's *Marketing Over Coffee*, there's *Social Toolkit*, *Freakonomics*, *Six Pixels of Separation*, *HBR IdeaCast*, *The Tim Ferriss Show*, and many more.

In short, podcasting is indeed on the rise—just don't expect it to be a meteoric one. And, maybe that's a good thing.

Presentations

SlideShare, owned and operated by LinkedIn, is a particularly great resource for those who work in the B2B world. At last count, the site had 70 million users, with 41 percent of all of North American B2B marketers using SlideShare to distribute content. To date, more than 18 million presentations have been posted to SlideShare.

Jason Miller, a talented content marketer working at LinkedIn, embraces visuals and an unexpected, entertaining way of presenting to people when he's building a deck to upload on SlideShare. "I think of slides as comedy bits," Jason says.[12] "The more stuff you have on a slide, the less you know your subject." Jason's a self-described TED Talks nerd. By reading the book *Talk Like TED*, Jason found that analysis of the top 1,000 Talks yielded an interesting observation: Roughly 70 percent of the Talks were stories. "I know it's very clichéd to say you're a storyteller these days, but if you don't have a story, if you don't have some sort of angle to build around, you're going to be boring. And nobody wants to hear that." We'll have more on Jason later in the book. We think you'll like him.

Getting Quoted

Why, as someone interested in building your brand, should you bother to get quoted? Two reasons: name recognition and validation.

Name recognition is obvious. The more you're quoted, the more likely it is that people will come across your name. That's fine. But recognition alone isn't enough; you want to be known as having expertise in one way or another. If you get quoted by journalists or other experts, that helps validate you as an expert. Nobody wants to quote an idiot, and there's a general level of trust of journalists, bloggers, and the like that they've done their homework, and they're quoting you because you are credible.

Using HARO, Patreon, and Muck Rack

Help a Reporter Out, more commonly known as HARO, is a digital service designed for journalists and sources to quickly find one another. It's essentially a marketplace in which journalists can connect with individuals just like you, who have a particular expertise in one area or another, so that the media can get good information—and quotes—for stories they are working on. Founded as a Facebook group by entrepreneur Peter Shankman in 2008, it was eventually turned into a mailing list with upward of 100,000 members, and acquired by Vocus in 2010.

In case you think only small-time publications use HARO, relax: *The New York Times*, *The Huffington Post*, *Mashable*, ABC News, and many other top-shelf organizations have developed stories using sources they found through HARO.

Patreon is a crowdfunding platform based out of San Francisco. Created by musician Jack Conte and developer Sam Yam, it allows artists to obtain funding from patrons on a recurring basis, or per artwork. Artists simply set up an account so that patrons can offer up pledges of donations for each time the artist creates a piece of art. Patrons are able to set a monthly maximum threshold or a fixed monthly amount as an option as well. This is in contrast to Kickstarter, where artists only receive all donations if a campaign is successful; artists, regardless of their success, have to set up a new campaign each time they want support to back their next piece of art. Patreon does have something in common with Kickstarter: It is common for artists to provide thank-you rewards to their supporters.

The platform funds itself by taking a 5 percent commission on all pledges by patrons.

Nearly half of Patreon artists create YouTube videos; the rest are a diverse group of Webcomic producers, podcasters, writers, and graphic designers.[13] Though patrons donate only $7 on average per piece of art created, Patreon is seeing substantial growth, reaching 10,000 artists by February 2014.[14]

Muck Rack—a product of Sawhorse Media, the New York City–based company that is also responsible for the Shorty Awards—is designed to help public relations professionals, marketers, and journalists become more successful at building their brands. Journalists can use Muck Rack to build a portfolio of their articles, get contacts via the platform's robust database, measure their work's impact, stay on top of what colleagues are working on, and uncover new career opportunities. On the flip side, corporate marketers and PR practitioners can use the platform to pitch journalists relevant stories, monitor mentions of their personal and corporate brands, and track success of their awareness campaigns.

If you're looking to pitch something that you're working on directly, Muck Rack can be a big time-saver. You can create multiple media lists, adding relevant journalists to each list and including relevant notes based off of previous contacts to make your communication as targeted as possible.

Promoting Engagement vs. the Bystander Effect

You may have experienced the bystander effect, a well-documented phenomenon that occurs in emergency situations. Someone is getting robbed, or there's a car accident, or there's a fire—and nobody does anything. Why does that happen? It's not because people don't care; they're horrified or even in shock. It's because of the other people. Our immediate reaction is to assume that someone else will get involved. After all, with so many people around, certainly someone will come to the rescue, right? But everyone responds the same way, and nothing gets done. Nobody feels personally involved.

The same thing happens when you focus on mass channels of communication to try to build your brand. Impersonal form e-mails sent to 10,000 people "to whom it may concern" and address-less messages sent out into the ether of the Web are not going to be snatched up. Nobody who sees these things feels like it's targeted at them; surely the content creator expects others to respond, but not me, right?

One mistake that we've seen time and time again is that somebody rebrands themselves and, to save time, uses a business e-mail marketing platform such as MailChimp to send out a huge "e-mail blast" to, say, 500 individuals at once. That's pretty efficient use of your time, right? Well, maybe, if your goal is to have an e-mail that is technically lying in somebody's inbox. But last time we checked, that wasn't the goal. The goal is to inform people, solicit advice on the new direction, and perhaps get introductions that are relevant to your rebranding. E-mail blasts are not great at any of that because they are so impersonal. They might get opened 30 percent of the time and responded to 5 percent of the time. By contrast, a personalized note may get opened 85 percent of the time, and responded to 50 percent of the time. The goal here isn't to just save time; it's to get the maximum return.

Chapter 4

Branding on a
Platform-by-Platform Basis

This book is all about displaying yourself in a way that will help people find you and see you as appealing, so you have to spend some time developing your profile/persona. The content you seed each of your channels with should "match" in the sense that it should feel cohesive: conveying your expertise, showing your accomplishments, and displaying your personality in a manner that doesn't contradict itself. Everything you say on digital platforms should fit with how you present yourself offline, too. LinkedIn, for example, is a great place to display your career trajectory; you can show who you worked for, where you went to school, and a short summary of your expertise. It's also a good platform to see your network and if you know anyone connected to the job or company that you're looking at. Similarly, a person that you might have sent to your profile can see if you're connected to anybody who's a thought leader in your industry, any publications that you might have contributed to, and any groups that you might belong to.

It's important to take a look at all of the different touch points that someone might have with you, particularly digitally, and tweak accordingly. Even small edits to biographical copy can go a long way toward telling the story you are trying to tell. Let's say you're trying to position yourself as a leadership coach. You're 27, and you haven't personally managed that many individuals in your career, so you're concerned that people will be too focused on that. If you think back over your career to date, you might remember that you led a cross-functional group within your company that improved productivity by 30 percent. And yet, that fact might not be in your bio yet. Well, shouldn't it? Anything that helps you better tell your story should be included.

We have both spoken to people who are afraid of changing a phrase or two on their Website for fear that everybody will immediately notice the change and call them out on it. The reality is that people are busy, and aren't likely to notice these small changes or poke fun at you because of them.

As you make these changes, try to look at all the different places where you can reflect your new or updated branding. If you send out bios of yourself for speaking appearances, reread the copy to make sure that it is as up-to-date and relevant as possible. Rethink your e-mail signature. Look at your LinkedIn headline. Listen to your voice-mail recording, even, and see if it tells the story that you are trying to tell. Double-check, and then triple-check. This is especially important after moving to a new company, or moving into a new role at your existing company.

When you have completed your branding (or rebranding) process, you want to make sure that people notice these changes, and the best way to do so is to ensure that they meet the new you. This means being proactive in reaching out, via LinkedIn, e-mail, or phone, in person, and so on. Generally, try to think about which approach is most appropriate for each individual and is most likely to get the response that you would like. For a close friend who has morphed with time into a client, a less-formal approach is probably best; for a mentor 25 years your senior who always addresses you very formally, make sure to respond in kind.

Sprucing Up Your Digital Presence

Years ago, it wasn't that easy to build your own Website. Now, if you're serious about your career, there's pretty much no excuse. When developing your personal Website, make sure it includes or has a link to your CV, publications, patents, contact information, and any sort of content that makes you stand out. A solid Website is a good way to really get interest from a recruiter, from a company that might want to hire you, and just anyone who wants to see what you're capable of. It shows who you are professionally, displays your professional drive and what direction you're aiming for, and helps demonstrate your professional contributions to society.

For a simple landing page, consider About.me. It's a tool that doesn't overpromise, and is arguably the quickest way to build a Web presence. Sign up with About.me, and you'll receive a single landing page where you can add a photo that represents your brand, as well as a brief bio. Of course, you can include links to your social profiles and other Websites if you have any.

Flavors.me isn't that dissimilar to About.me. One difference is that it does let you embed videos and audio, making it a solid fit for professions such as graphic design and videography.

If you're thinking about building a full-featured Website, you could do a lot worse than Squarespace. It allows you to develop a sophisticated-looking, modern Website at very affordable prices. Although you can inject code to customize further, there's no need: You can complete your site without seeing a single dreaded HTML bracket. Most non-techies can use Squarespace's drag-and-drop editor to complete a site, making it ideal for photographers, entrepreneurs, artists, and small business owners who aren't interested in learning an ounce of code.

If you're not ready to launch, or if you're looking to acquire an audience, Launchrock is worth checking out. It's a very simple site builder that is focused on customer acquisition, so it's optimized for collecting e-mail addresses.

Above all, your content has to be consistently engaging. You don't need flashy, distracting banners (this isn't 1995, or GeoCities—remember that?), but you do need a design that will present your brand in a way that represents you well. You also need to avoid the mistake that many make by favoring quantity over quality. Quantity is obviously important, but quality is harder to come by these days, and will help separate you from the crowd.

Social Marketing Expectations

As you build your brand via social media, remember that it won't change your fortunes overnight, and won't develop itself without quite a bit of TLC. If you don't know what you're doing, you're just not going to get the kind of quick results you're expecting. It's fine if you're not adequately prepared to engage properly; that just means that a gradual entry into social media marketing is your best approach. Personal branding success is something that takes time and effort, and where social media is concerned, patience is not just a virtue—it's a necessity.

In the end, however, the results of a strong social media presence are well worth it. If you demonstrate that you are a brand worth engaging with, your digital presence will grow. You'll not only build an audience, but also meaningful relationships behind the numbers.

Developing the Perfect Social Media Mix

Much like a corporate brand, a personal brand needs to serve a purpose in order to succeed on social channels. It has to have something productive to say.

If you ask your audience for their thoughts in a way that conveys improving your brand will also benefit them, you'll get honest answers. Indicators such as comments, mentions, and shares all demonstrate engagement with your audience. That's what you want. But not all engagement is created equal, and you have to strive for more than just numbers. The most straightforward way to generate quality interactions is to post good content. That content, though, needs a purpose and should help you not only build your brand, but build it in the direction you're looking to go. If you want to be known as a scientific researcher, then post the latest scholarly article—or Neil deGrasse Tyson's latest bon mot—more often. It doesn't have to be 24/7, but if you're posting 20 percent of the time about scientific research and 80 percent of the time about competitive women's badminton, well, people will logically assume that you're primarily interested in sports, right?

Introverted? No Problem

Don't be afraid to be unorthodox: Other people who work in branding or marketing might downplay your strategy, but they're not the people you're trying to attract. You're trying to reach *your* audience, so what works for others might not be what's right for you. If you find a way to stand out, there's no question that you should take advantage of it.

Branding and marketing can prove tough for introverts. After all, many branding strategies are based on extroverted approaches to brand building. But some branding tools, such as social media, may actually be advantageous to introverts.

If you're on the introverted side of the spectrum, you can leverage your contemplative side through a blog. Blogs allow an author to take their time, get their thoughts in order, and engage with others in a way that's more comfortable for them—at a distance, and with less intimidation. Although you might not be as visible, you can work to build a powerful brand on the strength of your ideas—especially if you become adept at promoting your blog or even guest blogging for other sites. Of course, introverts don't have to blog to be successful; this category includes the likes of J.K. Rowling, Bill Gates, and Emma Watson.

Different Social Platforms;
Different Content Strategies

It is crucial to understand what sort of content and messaging will work in different social channels. On Twitter, it pays to be succinct. On Instagram, it's important to have stunning imagery, accompanied by great captions and relevant hashtags.

One thing to think about is your "signal-to-noise ratio," the amount of information vs. the amount of unnecessary distraction. This ratio of clear signal to white noise will depend on the quality of your content. To get your message across, you want as good of a signal as possible and as little noise as possible. Choose your words carefully, and make sure your message is a net positive.

Each social channel has its own types of messaging, and each one requires a different approach. If you don't personally use Facebook, LinkedIn, Pinterest, Twitter, Instagram, Snapchat, and others, then it will be difficult to get a sense of how each of those channels develops and evolves, and you won't know what's appropriate and what isn't on each channel. It's best to not only have a nominal understanding of the pros and cons of each platform as they evolve, but also to keep abreast of the latest news regarding each one of these channels. Reading publications like *The Next Web*, *Mashable*, and *ReadWrite* will help.

Focusing on Where Your Audience Is

Just like a business location in the physical world, you have to be where your digital audience is. Due to the sheer number of social networks and apps to investigate, you're better off engaging in fewer places more effectively, rather than trying to do a little bit of everything and spreading yourself too thin.

Ever get a bagel with cream cheese, only to find there's not enough cream cheese to really satisfy you? That's because it's spread too thin. Engaging on multiple platforms is fine, and often necessary, but if you overextend yourself as a brand then you're not satisfying anybody. Focus is a good thing, when you spend your time where your customers are.

If you don't know where *your* audience is, don't stress: There are tools that run searches that will tell you how much of your prospective audience is on a particular social channel. Services such as ManageFlitter and SocialBro are incredibly useful in searching Twitter tweets and bios to see if professionals relevant to your brand are engaging there. Likewise, you can use Facebook's Search function.

And remember, even if a platform doesn't seem to have the widest appeal, that doesn't mean it's not an opportunity for you. Although visually driven platforms such as Instagram and Pinterest have risen, Flickr remains somewhat popular with more visual niches such as photographers and makeup artists.

Using Google Analytics to Understand Your Audience

It's important to get feedback from others explicitly, but often that's not feasible. In cases like this, it makes sense to get implicit feedback as well. Google Analytics is a pretty great way to collect insights from your audience.

In case you've been living underneath a rock, Google Analytics is a free tool (oddly enough, from Google) that gives you great insights on your Website's audience. One of the things you can learn about your audience is their age. You might think that the average age of the people you're speaking to is 45–54, only to look at your analytics and uncover that 25–34 is the most dominant age group. That might affect the way in which you present content on your site. Another interesting observation is how your audience breaks down along gender lines. Firebrand had one client who was certain that women visited its Website more frequently than men, but Jeremy was able to show them that Google Analytics had estimated that 68 percent of their audience was, in fact, male.

Preferred language is another observation one can draw from looking at analytics. Now, if you speak American English, you won't be shocked to find out that it's the dominant group on your Website. However, you might be surprised to find out that 11 percent of your audience's de facto language is simplified Chinese. If you're a landscape architect open to international projects, you might want to consider adding a Chinese version of your Website, or at least key parts of it, for audience members like this. Offering a good, authentic translation is a respectful way of acknowledging that your culture isn't the only one out there.

Related to language is location—another key attribute that can be observed from Google Analytics. Although the majority of your visits will probably come from the United States if that's where you reside, you might uncover that 9 percent of your audience hails from France and another 8 percent from the Philippines. That's not insignificant, and it's worth figuring out why that is. It could be that your blog content is particularly relevant to the Philippines, in which case you might want to consider expanding your LinkedIn and Twitter outreach in that region.

If your business is almost exclusively national, that's okay: You can just see which individual cities are browsing your site. When looking at Firebrand Group's traffic, we see New York City as the top result, which is where we're based, followed by Los Angeles. But we also see some surprising ones such as Jacksonville, FL (#4), Poughkeepsie, NY (#8), and Federal Way, WA (#19), between Seattle and Tacoma. Now, if we weren't on top of our analytics, we wouldn't realize that a decent percentage of our audience is in Federal Way. This lets us do further research on the good people of Federal Way, try to establish which companies there are looking at us most often, and so on.

It's also important to analyze how people are browsing your site. Everybody says that they're designing "mobile first," meaning they're thinking about mobile design and user experience before they start obsessing over the browser experience. Identifying how your audience splits its time among mobile, desktop, and tablet is important.

But so is determining what kind of browser someone is using—such as Chrome, Safari, Internet Explorer, Edge, or Firefox. If the vast majority of people using your site are employing an old version of Internet Explorer, for example, that probably means your audience is less technically literate on the whole, and may be overwhelmed by your Website if you use too many cutting-edge features.

If you want to get very technical, Google Analytics even lets you do custom reporting. This is powerful stuff that lets you create mashups of different types of metrics to really get under the hood and understand your customers. For example, when writing this, we put together a custom report that let us see the average amount of time people from different countries are spending on the Firebrand Group site. From this, we can see that people from the U.S. spend an average of 55 seconds (30th overall), with the most attentive viewers being from Venezuela, at an average of 5 minutes, 17 seconds apiece. Thank you, Venezuela! We look forward to seeing those speaking invitations roll in.

By the way, when you go to "Custom Reporting," there's a relatively new "Import from Gallery" feature that is incredibly useful. It lets you import any reports and dashboards that have previously been created by Google Analytics gurus, or ninjas, or whatever you want to call them, from around the world. (Tip: Don't call anyone a ninja, especially yourself, if you want to be taken seriously.)

Securing the Right Real Estate for Your PB Platform

Reserving your brand name is something you'll want to take care of early on. If your name is Harvey Sourpuss, for example, you'll want to grab Harveysourpuss.tumblr.com and so on. Identify the social channels you think you'll be most active on, and grab your spot. Facebook, Twitter, YouTube, and most other digital platforms let you create accounts for free, so there's no excuse for not planting your flag.

Of course, generic or popular names might make it difficult to get the same account name across multiple channels. In order to prevent this, it would be a good idea to create an account name that you can use without fear of being beaten to the punch.

If you have a very common name, such as John Smith, you might try to get Facebook.com/johnsmith, but there's a good chance someone already has it. Jeremy, in particular, has a pretty common name; you'd be surprised at how many Jeremy Goldmans live in New York City alone. If someone has already laid claim to your preferred real estate, consider adding your middle initial to your digital channels consistently. So, rather than going by "John Smith" whenever possible and "John Q. Smith" when you have to, bite the bullet and go by the latter on a consistent basis. This will make it more likely that people will search for you using your middle initial, and be less likely to find that other John Smith, Guam's most famous hermit fly fisherman.

Don't overlook the growth of emerging platforms such as Snapchat and YikYak that could easily be the next big thing, as well as smaller platforms that could be useful for your specific niche. Although it may seem like an issue that you can easily put off for a while, reserving your brand name on emerging platforms prevents you from having to pry your brand away from someone else a few years down the line.

Small details matter. For instance, one way to improve your Facebook page is to set your URL to something much more user friendly. Facebook.com/BrandName is much more marketable than something like *http://www.Facebook.com/pages/ not-so-user-friendly/5758787367.*

Your username is not the only thing you need to standardize across all channels; your visuals are pretty important as well. Make sure your visual identity is consistent across all social channels that you consider to be part of your brand strategy. Creating these singular and recognizable touches across all your social channels will help your brand look legitimate. If you're a smaller player, this step is crucial to establishing yourself.

But visuals only have to remain consistent if you have the same goal across all platforms. Sometimes you're going to be using different platforms for different objectives. Jeremy used to use Instagram to post advertisements and marketing campaigns he found interesting—essentially, the visual version of his Twitter feed. However, he noticed that when he posted pictures of his daughter, pets, or food he had eaten out or prepared at home, he tended to get considerably more engagement. Bit by bit, he turned his Instagram feed over to this type of content. Though set to public, his feed is now so overwhelmed with non-business content that it's clear to all who follow him what to expect—or not to expect—from his Instagram. So yes, it is okay to use different platforms for different purposes.

Personalized Shortened Links

You'll often see short links that, when clicked, redirect you to other content with other URLs. One of the most prominent short URLs is bit.ly. Another is hubs.ly, used by Hubspot. Ow.ly links are from Hootsuite, whereas t.co means a link is being shortened by Twitter.

What's the point of all these short links? Well, for one, Twitter has a limit on the number of characters per tweet. This made people start gravitating to short URLs, in order to fit more content into their tweets. In fact, this is why Twitter introduced t.co links, to automatically shorten any long links that users wanted to share via Twitter. However, there are other advantages to these short links. For one, most link-shortening services provide built-in analytics on who has clicked them. For example, Jeremy used the link *bit.ly/1vcRx8n* to redirect social media users to "7 SlideShares to Power Your 2015 Growth," a Firebrand Group Insights article actually housed at *http://firebrandgroup.com/7-slideshares-to-power-your-2015-growth/*.[1] Any bit.ly link displays its analytics when adding a + to any bit.ly URL. So, *bit.ly/1vcRx8n+* indicates how many clicks that link has received (45 when we last checked), where the clicks were received (22 via Facebook, 18 from Twitter, and 5 unknown), and these tweets' geographic distribution (84 percent from the U.S., with a smattering from other countries). The analytics page will also show you the time distribution of clicks, so it's easy to see that 33 of the 45 clicks came in the link's first two days of existence.

Now, it's not all that difficult to purchase a branded short domain. Corporations do it all the time. Virgin has virg.in, Beats by Dre uses beats.is, *The New York Times* favors nyti.ms, and so forth. Should your personal brand follow suit?

One tool we love using for finding short URLs is *https://domainr. com*. So, if Jeremy was interested in getting a personally branded URL, he might use Domainr to find jer.my. Or, if he was interested in showing that he was a digital expert, he could go with digit.al. There's a pretty big price range among these domains, especially if they're being offered from international registrars. For example, .my and .al belong to Malaysia and Albania, respectively. They're technically "gettable" but international domains sometimes have specific requirements.

You can use a service such as Bitly to manage your branded short domain to drive your personal brand. It's been suggested that branded URLs lead to higher click-through rates, as the person potentially clicking is more likely to click if they recognize where the link originated from.

Is it worth it to have a short URL? There's no right answer. The truth is, many strong personal brands don't use them, but that actually makes those that use them stand out even more. We advocate looking at the cost, and making an educated assessment about how often you'll be using your personal link shortener. If you curate content as often as Jeremy does, it might be worth it. However, if you're primarily working behind the scenes and not sharing links that often, as in Ali's case, then you probably don't need to invest in that area.

3 Reasons Why Your Social Media Strategy May Not Be Working

You probably wouldn't be surprised to learn that three in four consumers rely on social media[2] to influence their purchasing decisions, or that eight in 10 are also influenced by their friends' posts. As a result, getting your social media game right is key.

It can be argued that, from a digital standpoint, a brand is only as good as its social media strategy. Think about it: You can have the most compelling content out there, but it's pointless if it doesn't reach the right audience. Having a solid plan to execute your business goals is essential. Despite their best efforts, some people never reach their full potential due to an inefficient approach. If your social media strategy is falling short, it may be because:

1. **You're using the wrong social media platforms.**

   Depending on your area of focus, not every social media outlet will be right for you. If you own or manage a restaurant, you're going to want to utilize Instagram or Pinterest to showcase your recipes and give viewers an idea of the overall dining experience, as well as considering an investment in Yelp to drive foot traffic. If you own a digital marketing agency, and you're constantly putting out industry-relevant white papers, LinkedIn and SlideShare might be the most relevant platforms to focus on.

   Spreading yourself too thin across all social media channels is a common mistake made by most social media managers. A more effective strategy is to pick the top three channels where you receive the most traffic and focus your attention there.

2. **Your social strategy does not support your business objectives.**

   Katie Roberts of Walden University said it best: "Having 300,000 Facebook fans is *not* a business objective."[3] It's true. 300,000 Facebook fans will not keep the lights on. However, 15,000 highly engaged fans very well could. It's not about the Likes; it's about the love—and the attention—that you can foster for your brand.

So before you engage, think about your business objectives, and work backwards to develop your social media strategy. Ask yourself: What is your brand's mission? What do you want your personal brand to accomplish in the long term? Every brand needs well-defined values and goals to serve as the compass that directs its strategy. Your activity on social media has to reflect your business goals. If you're opening a bakery and your goal is to make the most delicious and healthy cupcakes (if you incorporate kale, we're unfollowing you on Instagram), you have to use social media to tell your audience what makes your cupcakes unique and emphasize the value you place on both taste and health.

3. **Your expectations are unrealistic.**

Sometimes things *are* working, and you just haven't noticed. Let us explain.

We often get requests from potential clients to duplicate the results of a dominant digital brand—but on a shoe-string budget and within three months. There's an old adage that if you want something fast, cheap, and good, you can only expect two of the three. You can't become the next *BuzzFeed* overnight. The "don't set the bar too high" rule can apply to different areas of your life, but it's especially true when it comes to growing your business. Though you may be putting in a lot of time and effort, don't expect to see exceptional results right away. The same is true for budget: Don't fall for the old "social media is free" myth. Make sure you've budgeted properly for social media success, and even then, give yourself some wiggle room, as social media-related manpower and advertising costs are on the rise.

Just take a deep breath, and understand that it takes time. As long as you maintain steady growth, you are on the right track.

Using Different Social Platforms to Reach Your Audience

Facebook and Twitter are the classic social media and branding tools: They can reach a lot of people quickly, they're user-friendly, and they are well established. But there are many other tools that you may be underutilizing in your personal branding arsenal.

Pinterest, for example, allows you to show your ideas in an innovative context in order to create awareness, as well as to communicate your values and reinforce your brand identity. You can also find out about your target audience; by tracking user interests and trends, you can identify what matters to the people you want to engage with.

Pinterest requires more time and effort than a quick one-line Facebook post or tweet, but it allows you to have a deeper dialogue with your audience. This in-depth way of managing your digital persona shows people that you care enough to go that extra mile, and it gives your media efforts depth as well as breadth.

LinkedIn is the premier social networking site for business. It tends to be used by the most digitally savvy professionals regardless of age. Therefore, you may find it to be one of the most important Web locations for presenting your personal brand. In addition to networking itself, LinkedIn allows users to post articles, which can help you create content to back up your message. The platform is built for the purpose of visibility, credibility, and connect-ability, and is a great resource for anyone looking to best represent their digital persona. We'll discuss LinkedIn in greater depth in a few chapters.

The Importance of a Great Photo

Your profile photo needs to convey a sense of trust. First off, you should have a photo, period. Not having a photo up on your Twitter, Facebook, LinkedIn profile, and so on is a sign that you're behind the times. Assuming you do have a photo up, it should be appropriate to the type of persona you're trying to convey. If you are a financial executive trying to convey your professionalism, choose a photo where you're wearing business attire and looking the part. On the other hand, if you are in a creative field—and are known for being a bit quirky—a sense of humor or informality in your photo might be appropriate. Your photo should be very well aligned with your persona.

It's likely that you maintain different types of connections on different platforms, in which case it's fine to have a different profile photo on each platform. That way, you can give a sense of who you are to the people you connect with on that platform. At the same time, if you do use all social networks for similar purposes, consider investing in a well-lit, attractive headshot that you can use across all of your key platforms.

Fun fact: A lot of people don't realize that privacy settings should be taken seriously. We have seen many people who do a good job of setting their Facebook privacy settings, with the exception of their Facebook profile photo, which is set to public for all to see. If you've chosen a risqué or inappropriate Facebook profile photo, make sure you know who can see it.

What Types of Links Should You Be Sharing?

Any links that you share across your social platforms need to satisfy two different objectives:

1. Does this portray me in the way I'd like to be seen?
2. Does this add value for my followers?

You've got to remember that personal branding is not all about you. It's not just about what you want to share—it's about what other people want to read and what they want to pass along to their audiences.

There are great tools that will allow you to automate some of your link-sharing. Having access to free and easy to use tools like this, however, means that millions of others have access to those same tools. The people who succeed don't just put all of their social media on autopilot; the people who win are those who use tools like this properly. When you use a marketing automation tool properly, your engagement can become very efficient, and you can spend more time building relationships with your audience using the time that you have saved. If you use marketing automations tools in the wrong ways, you can annoy people and detract from your brand.

Buffer

Buffer is a fantastic content management platform for your social media content. Once you sign up for a Buffer account, whenever you find some good content that you don't want to share immediately, just place it in your buffer. You can create a schedule so that every single day, a certain number of times per day, your social media content that you've saved before will go out through Buffer. This way, you can build your audience by curating great content on an ongoing basis either from others or sharing good news about your own business.

Feedly—and Finding Great Content

There are a number of ways to find great content to share. One of the best tools to use to find relevant links is Feedly, an RSS aggregator that lets you subscribe to many different sites at the same time. Don't worry; you don't need to know anything about RSS in order to use Feedly. It lets you quickly rifle through article headlines and excerpts to figure out what you should be reading and considering sharing.

You create a number of different topics that you're interested in, go to different Websites, grab their RSS feeds, and then plug them into Feedly. You can also use Feedly's search tool to look for certain publications, such as *Mashable* or *Women's Wear Daily*, and then plug their feeds into Feedly so that you can quickly see all the different headlines from that publication and figure out which ones you want to read or possibly share with your social networks. Obviously, this is a great way to build your audience by creating a relationship and establishing yourself as somebody who's credible within the relevant industry.

You can create content categories and organize all of the different Websites that you subscribe to. Before you choose to share an article yourself, Feedly even lets you see how many shares each article has already received, giving you a sense of "social proof" that others have found an article useful. With Feedly, it's easy to import new sites to keep on your radar; simply hit the "Add Content" button and pick a Website or topic you are interested in.

When we find an article in Feedly that we're interested in reading, we click on it to get a preview of the article and some of the related images. But the thing that we both like best about Feedly is probably the fact that there are so many different options in terms of what you can do with the contents afterward. You can e-mail it to yourself or to other people, you can send it to Instapaper or Evernote and be working with some of those tools in a second, and you can send it directly to Twitter, Facebook, or Buffer.

Find quotes that are relevant to you, that really speak to you, and that reinforce your own personal brand. One Website we really like to find quotes like this is BrainyQuote.com. But there are definitely plenty of other sites where you can find this type of content. Now, when repurposing the content of others, make sure to use proper attribution. You should do this with anything you use on your social channels or Website. But if you have access to a graphic designer, one of the cool things you can do here is you can actually create a graphic featuring the quote, lightly brand it with your own colors, and then actually put that out on social media.

However, if you're going to do that, we definitely recommend getting the timing right. In 2013, when a power outage halted the Super Bowl for 34 minutes, Oreo jumped in with a timely tweet during the hiatus: "Power out? No problem." The message, coupled with an image captioned, "You can still dunk in the dark," was retweeted more than 10,000 times in an hour. The message, which had to have been put together on the fly, might just have grabbed more attention than Oreo's official million-dollar Super Bowl ad. That's how important it is to be topical.

7 Common Digital Persona Mistakes

It goes without saying that a strong social media presence is essential to the success of any business. Being a good community manager is both an art and a skill, and although some people have a knack for it, most go through a trial and error period to learn what works and what doesn't. There are many different components involved in successfully managing your brand's digital presence. As a personal brand, there's a good chance you'll be your own community manager, making these lessons very relevant to you:

1. **Failing to have a cohesive strategy.**

   Being organized is one of the most important qualities of an effective community manager. Not only is an overarching strategy essential, but your day-to-day posts require a thought-out tactical plan. Before you launch a campaign—such as announcing your new service, or appearing on the local news—it's crucial to have a step-by-step outline of how you plan to promote it. Too often, campaigns fall apart because one step wasn't fully thought out. Beat up your plan before putting it into action; that's far better than having someone else beat it up after it's already out in the open. Also, make sure that anyone else involved knows his or her role.

2. **Posting too much.**

   Nobody likes a spammer—and if you do like spammers, we encourage you to reexamine your life choices. In any case, posting too much is the quickest way to turn off your readers, and excessive posting lowers the value of each post. This is especially true on Facebook, but is relevant for other platforms as well. We've even run tests suggesting that posting a "B-level" asset immediately after an "A-level" asset will net the grade A piece of content less engagement through its lifetime.

Being more selective with your posts will allow you to invest more time and effort into making each one stand out, and it will also keep your audience more engaged—which is, of course, the goal of posting in the first place.

3. **Forcing it.**

No one's social media efforts have an A+ record. Just like in baseball, it's impossible to hit a home run every time. There will inevitably be campaigns that don't perform well, and when this happens you simply need to accept it. Don't make the common mistake of wasting more time and energy on something that is clearly not resonating with your audience. Instead, perform a post-mortem to figure out why the post or entire campaign didn't work, and what lessons can be learned for next time.

4. **Spreading yourself (and your brand) too thin on social platforms.**

You can't be everywhere at once, so don't stress yourself out trying to promote your brand across every platform. Instead, you should target two or three where you are likely to get more readership and engagement; determining which platforms will largely depend on your audience's demographics. We see this proven out time and time again: A brand breaks its time investment out relatively equally among, say, seven different platforms— even though the majority of the value generated comes from one or two of those. If you were dating seven people at once, wouldn't you eventually phase out the less-promising prospects so you could give more attention to the most appealing? The same principle applies here.

While on the topic of spreading yourself too thin, make sure you enlist the help of your key constituents to ensure your campaigns get the attention they deserve. Trying to do it all alone will only lead to burnout, poor results, or both.

5. **Trying to please everyone.**

Trying too hard to be likeable can often backfire. It's impossible to make *everyone* like you, and this real-life principle absolutely applies to digital marketing. As your brand grows, and more people are reading your content, negative comments are unavoidable. In fact, some (not all, but some) audience members get off on being trolls. If you take this type of feedback personally and get defensive, it will wipe you out emotionally. The smarter course of action is to do your best to address the problem, learn from it, and move forward.

6. **Being a selfish promoter.**

If you are only promoting your content and aren't taking the time to support other professionals in your network, chances are slim that others will help you spread the word about your campaigns. Also, it's important to recognize the difference between actively engaging (participating in conversations, retweeting relevant content, and so on) and promoting like a used car salesman (indiscriminately hijacking hashtags, caring more about your promotion than what customers can get out of it). You know that "friend" who only reaches out when they need a favor? Don't be that guy.

7. **Focusing on quantity, not quality.**

Many social media managers make the mistake of dwelling on the number of Twitter followers and Facebook likes and comments, rather than paying attention to who their visitors actually *are*. This is an easy trap to fall into; total Likes on your Facebook page is easy to track, yet it's a metric that's becoming increasingly meaningless. A smaller, loyal following is twice as valuable as a large audience that doesn't care about anything you have to say.

Building Your Visibility

Regardless of platform, it is beyond important that you create an effective profile that is easily searchable, and that presents your brand as authentic. Ultimately, we're talking about making you more *visible*. But what makes up visibility? When you think about it, the idea of visibility can seem like a vague concept, so you have to have specific goals in mind when trying to increase your impact.

To get you started, decide what you want to be, and how you want to look. These ideas will provide you guidance in all your activities, and give you direction as you develop your brand.

Find out where your current audience is coming from. As we mentioned, there are tools you can use to measure the amount of traffic going to your Website, blog, or social profiles. For example, when it comes to your Website—and sometimes your blog—you're able to easily insert a bit of code that gives you access to the basic version of Google Analytics, a free toolkit that will identify the geographic location of your visitors, what sites they originated from, and many other helpful bits of data. Although you can't get perfect information about who is visiting your social profiles, you are able to use link-shortening services, such as Bitly or Tiny URL, to direct people to your profiles. These shortened links can provide some analytics about who is clicking.

Of course, the odds of increasing your visibility are greatly enhanced if you get connected to others. This doesn't just mean your audience, but your peers as well: You stand to get far more if you reach out and take action to build your network of connections. Your strategy needs to include a concerted effort to grow your contacts, which, in turn, will grow your potential audience.

Establish a solid, central place for people to find you. Though it does help to be active on multiple mediums, having one recognizable and well-known platform on which people can contact you can help in at least a couple of ways:

- 👍 It provides a location for people to post questions or comments, providing feedback and ideas from others.
- 👍 It helps people who share similar interests in your industry or profession to find you.

One way to grow your contacts more rapidly is to go to networking events and meet like-minded people who you'll want to know later. More on that in Chapter 8!

Above all else, if you're going to be presenting your brand to other people, particularly those who have experience in your field, you have to know your brand inside and out. If you were writing a book, you would have to be able to explain what it is about in a way that makes people want to read it. Building a brand is no different. If you're not knowledgeable or excited enough about your brand, why should anyone else be?

Purchasing Fake Followers

Now, some people just want to purchase fake followers and be done with it. We get asked about this more often than you might think. The short answer to whether or not you should do it: no, absolutely not, avoid it.

For one, there are a number of tools that will let you spot a faker. One of these is Wildfire's Monitor (Monitor.wildfireapp.com), which can let you see historical spikes up and down on a specific Facebook page or Twitter account. If you see a major upward spike, there's a good chance that the account's owner purchased followers. (If there's a major downward spike, Facebook or Twitter noticed the fake followers and removed them.) Another useful tool is Fakers by StatusPeople (Fakers.statuspeople.com), which will scan the Twitter account of your choosing and analyze what percentage of its followers are fake and which followers are no longer active, and determine the true quantity of "good" followers.

Well-informed people will know if you purchase followers. There's a chance that you're going to confuse a few less digitally savvy individuals here and there by having fake followers, but it's ultimately not that hard to spot. So if you're looking to build your own personal brand, buy fake followers at your own peril.

Unfortunately, fake followers have become a real problem. Perhaps it's insecurity or maybe it's a need to look more famous than you are, but many big brands as well as personalities invest in fake followers. This isn't a good thing, and in fact, if you participate in this practice you might be doing yourself a disservice. It can be very embarrassing for you for all of your real followers to wake up one day and notice that you have lost 4,000 followers who were all robots. You don't want to become infamous for being inauthentic.

Some corporate brands invest in fake followers because they're looking to get funded, or appear to look as if they have a sense of momentum. We can definitely see the appeal of investing in some fake followers to bolster your personal brand, but it's a crutch. It's dangerous to trick yourself into thinking that you're doing a good job of building yourself when that's not the case. It's a lazy practice. And laziness is not the way to become the best possible version of yourself.

By the way, just because somebody has a ton of followers doesn't mean that they actually purchased them or acquired them intentionally. Rather, people who sell fake followers are invested in making sure that social platforms do not automatically delete their fake followers—so they have learned to have these bots follow real brands and personalities, such as Coca Cola and Ryan Seacrest, to name but a few examples.

Targeting via E-mail, CRM, and Facebook

Sometimes the old tricks are the best tricks. Customer relationship management (CRM) and e-mail marketing can be invaluable tools when trying to build your brand. E-mail might seem outdated, yet it can still be quite effective.

If you want to analyze the sizes of different market segments on Facebook, it's not that difficult to do some testing. You can go to *https://facebook.com/ads/create/* and fill in the mandatory fields to get past step 1. When you get to step 2, aka targeting, you select criteria that best describe your target audience. As you tweak what you are looking for, Facebook will automatically show you how many of its members fit that profile. Of course, this is not an exact science, but it does give a sense of how large your market is in relation to other potential business opportunities.

Using Facebook, you can engage with your audience using advertisements that are targeted to specific geographic locations, demographics, interests, and more.

Targeting and segmenting don't end with Facebook likes, however. The links, status updates, and photos you post can be tailored for specific countries, cities, and languages. As a result, you can craft a different message for each particular demographic in your global audience.

5 Underrated Pillars of Masterful E-mailing

It might be one of the least sexy skills on the planet, but the ability to weave a flawless e-mail is an enviable trait. Because so much of communication is derived from nonverbal cues such as body language, an effectively written e-mail is particularly important: Without those nonverbal cues, e-mails can so easily get misinterpreted, at best leading to minor misunderstandings, and at worst, derailing important business projects.

Depending on what type of job you hold, e-mail etiquette can vary significantly. In many corporate cultures, the tone is formal and messages are very matter-of-fact, whereas other companies are accustomed to informal interactions involving smiley faces and cute "xoxo" signoffs. But wherever where you work, one thing remains the same: Your e-mail manners matter.

Here are five general rules to follow to master the art of e-mailing:

1. **Be direct.**

   If your inbox is anything like Jeremy's, chances are it's flooded by a ridiculous number of e-mails per day. Given that, it's imperative that all your outgoing e-mails have a clear subject line. Also, in the body of the e-mail make sure you get to the point using as few words as possible. Lengthy messages typically scare more people off.

   "It's very simple; e-mails should deliver information and, if needed, send out a call to action," says Deb Merry, marketing expert and entrepreneur.[4]

   Speaking of delivering information efficiently: When a long e-mail exchange morphs into a new topic but the subject hasn't changed, it's time to edit the subject to make the thread easier to find in the future.

2. **Know your audience.**

   Lindsey Pollak, e-mail etiquette consultant and author of *Getting from College to Career* explains, "Your e-mail greeting and sign-off should be consistent with the level of respect and formality of the person you're communicating with."

   Lindsey advises writing "for the person who will be reading it—if they tend to be very polite and formal, write in that language. The same goes for a receiver who tends to be more informal and relaxed."[5]

   Before reaching out to any potential clients or customers, it's important to do your homework. In other words, you need to develop a mental image of who they are and what they'll respond to, and write your e-mail accordingly.

3. **Add a personal touch.**

   Adding a personal touch is usually very effective. For example, if you are reaching out to an author to request a book for reviewing, it's a good idea to compliment some of his previous work. Not only does it make him feel good, but it shows you put in the effort to learn about him. Who wouldn't want to do business with someone like that?

If you're using a tool like Salesforce or Contactually to send out a number of e-mails at once, be sure to personalize before sending. A mass mail that feels like a mass mail is a major turnoff.

4. **Follow up and express your gratitude.**

In many cases, your initial exchange will require a follow-up. It's one thing to establish a connection, but learning how to maintain relationships is another skill entirely. Following up after a pitch meeting? A short, unique e-mail showing your appreciation for the other parties' time will go a long way. Responding to press? Your follow up "could be as simple as a quick e-mail or tweet saying thanks, or it could be following up with feedback about the coverage," Crew Blog reports.[6]

Follow-up e-mails are a great opportunity to say thank you and leave on a positive note so you can continue doing business together.

5. **Don't just take—give.**

Whether you're following up with someone or just checking in with a contact you're out of touch with, it usually feels less obtrusive if you try to add value in some way. If there is a product they might be interested in, let them know. If there is news relevant to their industry, let them know. If you have a suggestion for their business that can help them improve their profitability—well, you get the idea.

You never want to be the type of contact who only gets in touch when you want something; that's a great way to keep your professional network small.

Chapter 5

Engagement

Getting Good at Listening

Listening to customers is one of the most important things you can do. If you're just broadcasting your own agenda, then you're missing out on the larger conversation. But passive listening—simply allowing your customers to speak without a response—isn't going to cut it, either. You need to engage in active listening, give your audience cues that you're paying attention, and work based on the feedback that they're providing. As you build your brand, active listening helps you begin a conversation and create more intimate connections.

You don't have to build your whole brand around what your audience wants, but you should have a good reason for not incorporating their feedback. Doing so without a compelling reason can have some significant consequences. If you don't respond to people, your audience is going to go elsewhere.

If you think you're a poor listener, you need to work on becoming a good one as soon as possible. Even if you think you're already a good listener, then you need to work on becoming a *great* listener. You can always improve, and the difference will stand out to your audience.

Finding People to Network With

One question we often field is, "How do I find the right people to engage with?" One of the best places for that purpose is Twitter, and one of our favorite tools for that platform is called ManageFlitter. If you're interested in being followed by CMOs at large organizations (which is the type of thing that Jeremy's interested in), you can go in and follow a whole horde of CMOs at the same time and then look to see which ones engage back. From that foundation, you can start to build authentic relationships over time.

Another tool that we enjoy using is called SocialBro. We really like the visual interface, and the wealth of tools it puts at your fingertips. Using SocialBro, you can look at everybody who's following you as well as everybody that you're following as one giant community. From that point, you can run some pretty sophisticated searches in order to find people who are worth building relationships with. For example, if you are in the financial industry and looking to move to New York, you might look for individuals who have the word "finance" in their bio, with "NYC" in the location field. You can also add a few other filtration qualifiers, such as looking for people who have more than 1,000 followers, who have tweeted in the last two months, with their account over four months old, and so on. You can then create Twitter lists based off of these sophisticated queries, and access them from the main Twitter interface or any third-party Twitter management tool such as Hootsuite or Sprout Social.

One of the best ways to network in your daily life is to join meetups and networking groups. If you want to be successful on digital platforms, you need to find the digital equivalent. Facebook Groups, Twitter Chats, and LinkedIn Groups are some of the best ways to network your way into a stronger personal brand.

Facebook Groups, if you aren't familiar with them, are an underrated and powerful part of Facebook. You can build a group focused on just about anything, or build your own. For example: Ali belongs to a couple of strength training groups, and several networking groups for creatives, while Jeremy has joined groups such as Social Media Managers, which as of this writing has 7,429 members. These groups function a little different than the rest of Facebook: Though you can post a status, photo, and video as you might usually do, it's also possible to post a question with multiple choice answers, or a file, which can be uploaded from your computer or Dropbox.

One of the best things about Facebook Groups is that Facebook algorithmically decides that content coming from your groups is highly likely to be relevant to you, so new group posts will usually show up prominently in group members' newsfeeds. This means if you post, there's a good chance most members will see it. Of course, you want to follow good etiquette, so don't try to be promotional too often. People won't click on your links or respond to your posts if they don't know you, so try to chime in on other peoples' posts whenever relevant. You don't want to jump in on a thread where you're underinformed, but it's good to find moments to add value when you can, as that will help build your reputation in the community.

Another useful vehicle for networking is Twitter Chats, which are virtual events housed on Twitter organized around a particular hashtag. Every participant uses the same hashtag to be included in the conversation. Twitter Chats are also typically moderated by someone or multiple parties, are focused on a specific topic, and last for a specific amount of time. Some chats are weekly; others, biweekly or monthly. Others are once-in-a-lifetime events.

When it comes to networking, definitely don't overlook LinkedIn. This platform also has a Groups feature; groups are searchable by interest and industry, and are a great way to meet new people who can help you build your brand. Groups provide a place for professionals in the same industry or with similar interests to share content, find answers, post and view jobs, make business contacts, and establish their industry expertise.

Group managers aren't typically picky about who they accept, but they do have the ability to review your request to join a group and make sure that you fit its membership criteria. Similarly, the group's owner or moderator gets to decide what type of content will be allowed; they can delete discussions and comments that they feel are detrimental to the group. Similar to other platforms, read and participate in existing discussions before starting your own so you have a good idea of what that specific group considers valuable.

When sharing content from other publications or even from LinkedIn Pulse's section, remember that you've got to keep it professional—and when it comes to being professional, nothing says the opposite more than spamming people. If you're not active in a group and you share a link, even if it's relevant to the group's discussions, you're going to be less likely to start a conversation or be seen as legitimate. In fact, someone who is active in a group who shares a slightly relevant link is more likely to start a conversation than somebody who is less active but submits an extremely relevant link.

How to Develop Content That Promotes Engagement

Earlier on, we talked about the importance of good content. Content development is important, but so is how you get it in front of your audience. If you post good content, but it doesn't get people involved, then your content isn't supporting your personal brand development. Equally important to the quality of your content is getting people to engage with it, such as commenting, sharing, and so on. Where and when you say it is just as important as how you say it.

It can be tough to kick-start engagement, because nobody wants to be the first to comment on a thread. But once you get that first person to interact with you, your engagement can quickly gain momentum. The first step in getting a good response is to post at the right time (more on this in a bit). From there, start with those closest to you: Use relationships within your community. Even reach out directly to people in order to let them know that you've posted a new piece of content that you'd love for them to engage with. Whatever you do, don't be spammy! If Ali posts an article about blogging to her Facebook feed, for example, she may look for three or four blogger friends who she sees are online and ask them to comment, but she won't ask her technophobe aunt in New Jersey who still shares her husband's e-mail address. The key here is relevancy.

Once you've established this foundation of brand advocates who engage with your content, others will be encouraged to join in. Use this tactic wisely, however, or else you risk looking desperate and alienating your top advocates. Ask yourself: Are you doing them a favor by alerting them, or are they doing you a favor by sharing? You want the former to happen much more than the latter.

By the way, when we're talking about engagement, we mean truly having people engage with your content. Actions that require more on their part should count for more. For example, Likes are okay, but they're also lazy. By that, we mean that they're so easy for your audience members to offer that they don't have high value. Comments are much better and more useful responses from the community, because they require more thought and effort. In order to foster commentary, your posts should be interesting, encourage more specific feedback, or, ideally, both. If you're having trouble getting this kind of feedback, you might be asking the wrong questions, using the wrong platforms, phrasing things in the wrong way, or posting at the wrong time. Or your audience is less engaged than you might have thought.

Content Calendar

In order to make sure you can successfully engage with customers after they've liked or followed you, you must develop a strategy in advance. That involves building out a content calendar. In order to get a good return on your social media investment, you should develop realistic goals and objectives, including a step-by-step plan for getting from point A to point B. Your content needs to progressively build on itself, and take advantage of momentum in order to get your audience involved.

Getting Engaged

Once you hit your stride with engagement and content creation, your audience will come to expect regular updates. Maintaining this reliability is crucial to upholding your reputation.

Getting the Like on your Facebook page, or a friend request on your personal profile, is only half the battle. When someone takes that action, all you know is that they liked you in some small way for at least one fleeting moment in time. You've got their attention, but now comes the hard part: holding it.

With the tenuousness of that attention in mind, it is important not to overload them with self-aggrandizing messages that are overly promotional. If you flood your audience's newsfeeds with your communications, they are going to un-like your page, unfollow you, and have negative associations with your brand. Nobody likes being nagged. To succeed, your brand must find a happy medium between quantity and quality. Push your content, but don't be pushy.

Even though we've stressed the need for restraint, that doesn't mean you should wait to engage with people until they engage with you. Strike while the iron is hot, and while you're still in the forefront of their minds.

Optimizing Your Engagement Schedule

Once your content is developed, you then need to determine the opportune time to get that content in front of your audience. The timing of a Facebook post may seem like a minor detail, but it's really an important factor in determining the post's success. The same is true for Twitter, LinkedIn, and other platforms. For example, posting during the workday will lead to poor reception, whereas the best response rates occur during peak hours: early morning (7 a.m. EST), after work (5 p.m. EST), and late night (11 p.m. EST). But these are general guidelines; the times that work best for your audience may vary. For instance, if you're a famous insomnia expert, you may be targeting a parliament of night owls, so your peak time would be way past midnight.

Your posts should come when your audience is most likely to have your brand or your subject matter in mind. If you're a personal trainer, you might consider posting something on a Sunday night about "the best time for busy people to work out," before your audience gets tied up with their weekly schedule. Finding the optimal time to post can really boost your audience reception.

Knowing How to Ask a Question

When asking your audience a question, you have to frame it in just the right way. Don't be afraid to ask in a simple, outright manner, such as "Like us if…" or "Care to comment…?" or "Tell us if you…" and so on. Details matter: Positioning *where* or *when* or *would* at the end of the post brings 15 percent more engagement than those same words buried in the middle of the post. But be wary of *why* questions, which are seen as more intrusive and require more effort to answer than *what* questions. Once again, these guidelines may vary for your own brand, so learn what works for you.

As you can see, engaging across all platforms is key. That being said, LinkedIn will be one of the most beneficial for building your brand, which we'll cover in detail in the next chapter.

Chapter 6

Using LinkedIn to Its Fullest Capacity

Building Your Brand Using LinkedIn

"The résumé was paramount, with LinkedIn on the side. But now, it's just as important."[1] That's coming from Alyssa Gelbard, the noted career expert and president of Resume Strategists, a New York–based firm that positions its clients for long-term career success. Alyssa's rationale for LinkedIn surpassing the traditional resume is sound: "I may *send* you a résumé or it will be given to you, but anyone can find you or search you out on LinkedIn. Also, you can provide much richer information like a link to your book, or client reviews, or media clips. People are looking for you and you don't realize it." She's right: The average time spent reading a résumé is just 30 seconds. When it comes to searching for job candidates, companies primarily use Google and LinkedIn instead of job boards or talent databases. Furthermore, many companies are even requiring that new applications be screened using Google. If the first page of your Google search results isn't impressive, hiring managers may not even glance at your application.

For the reasons listed above and many others, LinkedIn is most likely the single best tool you'll have at your disposal to build your own brand. We want to shed light on LinkedIn's top personal branding features:

1. **Comment on your LinkedIn feed.**

   Your connections are posting articles, commenting on the activity of others, and starting group discussions—and what's great is that you can see all of this from your main LinkedIn feed. This provides a perfect opportunity to inject yourself into conversations, just like we discussed in the last chapter. Of course, only do this when you have something to say, such as an answer to someone's question, a follow-up question of your own, a congratulations of some sort, and so on. Don't just hit the Like button. That's lazy. Ever have a friend say "Hey, you should meet so and so! She's awesome. She likes my social media updates all the time"? Yeah, neither have we. Liking someone's activity is a lazy form of engagement, and won't get you any type of recognition or build your brand in any meaningful way.

2. **"Pulse recommends this news for you."**

   You know who succeeds in life? People who make the right moves. You know who makes the right moves? People who are well-informed. The business world is moving more quickly than ever, so if you don't read, there's a good chance you'll miss out. LinkedIn Pulse (*https://linkedin.com/pulse/*) is a great way to keep abreast of what's going on in areas that are most likely to be of interest to you.

3. **See who's viewing your profile.**

   Seeing who's viewing your profile is helpful, because you can get a better sense of what audience you're attracting. LinkedIn can give you insights, such as that 45 percent of your viewers have the title salesperson. So if your goal is to attract television producers, you can revise the keywords in your profile to start getting noticed by a more relevant audience.

You can also see how you rank in relation to others. At present, Jeremy ranks in the top 21 percent for profile views among professionals like himself. The nice thing about this is that it gives him a sense of how well he's doing at promoting himself on LinkedIn compared to others. Another plus is he can see professionals in similar fields who are doing even better, and learn from their examples. Often, we have used the "Professionals like you" list to find individuals who don't directly compete with us, and have the potential to become future allies.

4. **Add skills.**

When you're editing your LinkedIn profile, you can edit the list of skills you possess. This is helpful, as LinkedIn will often prompt your connections to endorse their connections' proficiency in various skills. Which means you, Milton Butters, can add the skill juggling to your profile. Then, your connections will occasionally be asked: "Does Milton Butters know about juggling?" and they'll have the option to hit the "Endorse" button. The more endorsements you get for that skill, the more people will think you're a lean, mean juggling machine, and all those juggling recruiters will beat a path to your door.

5. **Add an eye-catching headline.**

When you're deciding what to focus on with respect to your LinkedIn profile, start with what comes up first, beginning with the top of your profile.

"One mistake many people have made is putting a headline that doesn't *tell* anybody anything," shares Alyssa. "If you say you're president of Whatever, Inc., that doesn't mean anything to anybody. But 'chief strategist at [company name here]' or 'head of business development,' or something along those lines is useful. Give me something so I can tell who you are. VP/manager/director doesn't really tell me anything."

Headlines are incredibly important to your LinkedIn profile. After all, they sum you up in a nutshell. If the first thing you want people to know about you is that you're a keynote speaker, well, that absolutely belongs in the headline. If you are actively exploring new opportunities, that's the kind of thing you need to consider putting in the headline as well.

As for your company, if it's not commonly known among your intended audience, include a short but detailed description so your audience can see exactly what the company's focus is. Although plenty of professionals know what Firebrand Group does, Jeremy doesn't want to take for granted that his audience will necessarily know that it is an agency devoted to making marketing suck less, with a focus on digital strategy and branding.

6. Have a great summary.

One of the most important things about your LinkedIn profile is your summary. People will read your headline, and if you've enticed them into reading your profile, the #1 thing they'll read is your summary. The #2 thing is… there is no #2. But #3 is maybe, maybe, everything else in your profile. That's how important the summary is.

So, what should your summary say? Think of it this way. If you were introducing yourself to someone, and you only had 15 seconds, what would you want to have gotten out of your mouth before you run out of time? If you live and breathe museum research, you've got to make sure to relate that immediately in your summary. If you happen to have a Pez candy dispenser collection that is unrivaled in the entire country, which is interesting but in no way is something you think defines you professionally, then maybe leave that out. You can always list your National

Pez Council membership in the Affiliations part of your profile, anyhow.

Some people write their summary in the first person, and some people write it in the third person. Either way is fine. Personally, we think that writing in the third person is a little obnoxious. It makes it sound like you're too awesome to write your own LinkedIn profile. Part of the nice thing about social media is that it makes people more relatable. If you're trying to be *unrelatable*, then go ahead and write it in the third person.

7. **Notify your network of changes.**

When making changes to your profile, LinkedIn has a nice option that reads, "Yes, publish an update to my network about my profile changes." Generally speaking, you want to update your network when there are updates to your profile to maximize your visibility. LinkedIn sends out a daily e-mail to all of its members by default, unless they've opted out of these notifications, so updates will be published here.

We've seen some people play games by updating their profile daily, making obnoxiously minor changes just to show up in daily e-mails. You know who we're talking about. You might even be doing this. Stop it. It's like the boy who cried wolf; people will tune you out if you update too often. Instead, try to raise your visibility at key moments.

8. **Get recommendations.**

Getting recommendations on LinkedIn is one of the most underrated things you can do. Unlike endorsements, which are your connections' ways of saying you're good at specific skills, recommendations are completely free-form. Your colleagues can write as much or as little as they want.

Of course, people have to love you to spend five minutes crafting a nice note about you. Many profiles have zero recommendations. To improve your odds of getting a few of your own, why not write some recommendations for those you hold in high esteem? After all, it's better to give than receive. Once you write a recommendation for others, LinkedIn will ask if you want to send them a brief note asking for one in return. We think that's okay. While you're at it, why not guide your connections in the right direction? When requesting a recommendation, you can mention some of the attributes that you're looking to emphasize. If you're working in a scientific laboratory and looking to pivot into strategy consulting, you can request recommendations highlighting your decision-making, strategic mind, and consulting-relevant projects you have previously tackled.

We recommend giving people options. Don't just say you want recommendations purely focused on your ballet skills. If the person you're asking for a recommendation has never seen you do a plié, promenade, or pirouette, they might not feel comfortable giving you a ballet-related recommendation. Instead, give them roughly four things you want to be known for, which gives them options without boxing them in.

9. **Use a picture.**

Elsewhere we've covered the do's and don'ts of good social media pictures, but one thing that we notice often on LinkedIn—which annoys us to no end—is when people post pictures that are way too small for LinkedIn's dimensions. Make sure that you view your profile from both a phone and a browser to ensure that you've optimized it for all types of devices. You've put too much effort into your LinkedIn presence not to.

While you're at it, don't put up the wrong picture. Don't put up a picture of Mr. Whiskers, even if he is the favorite of your six cats. You have a new human baby? That's great. We're really happy for you. But it's not going to be your LinkedIn picture—even for a day. Not if we have something to say about it.

10. LinkedIn Groups.

We just talked about LinkedIn Groups in the last chapter, but they're important enough to warrant a mention here. Just like IRL (in real life), communities are important—and Groups are LinkedIn's version of communities. It's simple: If you participate in groups, you'll develop more lasting connections and you'll also bolster your reputation. If you don't participate at all, you're just not using LinkedIn to its fullest potential.

Now, using Groups takes time. It's understandable if you don't think you have the time to use them consistently. If you feel like you might get some value out of Groups, however, we would recommend setting up small chunks of time to check in and see if there are any threads that are interesting to you. You don't even have to set aside that much time. Maybe 10 minutes, twice a week. How does that sound? Don't tell us you can't do that.

The other great thing is that a lot of people have their settings set so that group members can send them a note and start a private conversation. If there's somebody you want to connect to, you can look on their profile and see what groups they're part of. Then you can join those groups specifically to send that person a message and say, "Hey, I noticed we're in the same group. I'd love to chat about...." Is that a little sneaky? Absolutely. But if you genuinely do have an interest in common, it's not that reprehensible.

When joining groups, it's important to find communities that have a highly active membership. You don't want to join a group and attempt to start a lively discussion and then find out that you're talking to yourself. You also might be tempted to drop a link to your most recent project and ask people to circulate it immediately, without building relationships in that group. This is not going to work. It's just like anywhere else: You have to build a relationship before you can ask people to do something for you. And this is the type of thing that all of us know in real life is true. But for some reason, when people start engaging online, they forget this really obvious fact. Because of that, we definitely recommend finding a few groups that are relevant to you, getting active in the discussions there, and building great relationships. People will be interested in commenting on a relevant post in the group as long as you do it in a less-than-spammy way.

11. LinkedIn Publishing.

LinkedIn's publishing tool is another way to build your personal brand and get in front of a lot of the right people. When you log in, you have the option to publish a post. But before you dive in, we recommend taking a look at the types of posts that are successful on LinkedIn so that you don't spend time developing content that won't work for your LinkedIn audience.

Some LinkedIn "Don'ts" to Avoid

Whether you're an avid social media user or a more casual browser, it's likely that you've come across a status or two that made you roll your eyes. Or maybe you've read a post that left you wondering, "What were they thinking?" If there's one platform where you should be especially mindful of your behavior, it's LinkedIn.

When it comes to branding yourself, remember that little things sometimes represent a lot. If you display your name in all lowercase, or you have typos in a key part of your LinkedIn profile, it's going to detract from your presentation. Likewise, if you're simply trying too hard to be witty or whimsical, that can hurt, too.

Of course, what may turn some people off may be attractive to others, and it's impossible to make everyone like you. Still, there are some things that experts generally recommend you stay away from, such as keyword stuffing. "Don't add keywords indiscriminately just to show up in more searches," advises Alyssa Gelbard. "If you're in accounting and use marketing terms, but your profile doesn't back it up, you've just wasted someone's time, and they'll automatically ignore you."

Here are a few additional LinkedIn "don'ts" to stay clear of:

1. **Don't collect connections just for the sake of it.**

   LinkedIn connections are not Pokémon: You don't have to catch them all. However, if you see someone interesting in your network and you want to connect with them, the best strategy is to join a group they're in, introduce yourself, and contribute to the discussion, as we mentioned earlier. Once you have established a presence in the group, you can invite them to connect with you. Make sure to explain why you'd like to connect so you don't come across as spammy or generic. We are much more likely to connect with someone if they mention something that is relevant to our interests rather than the default "I'd like to add you to my professional network on LinkedIn."

   If you have a connection in common, you can also ask them to make an introduction, but make sure that you know the mutual acquaintance well enough that it doesn't feel like an imposition. Leave them an out by making it easy to decline just in case they don't feel comfortable introducing you.

2. **Don't flirt.**

   This isn't Tinder. Flirting with coworkers in an office environment is inappropriate, and the same rule applies on LinkedIn. But though this might seem like common sense, it actually doesn't go without saying. Unfortunately. Somebody might look so compelling and attractive in their profile that you want to send a flirtatious message. But that wouldn't be appropriate in a workplace environment or an in-person networking event, so keep communications professional, not personal.

Online harassment is a huge issue, and one that should be taken seriously. It doesn't matter how eye-catching someone's profile pic is: If they want a date, they'll post their profile on a dating site. Behavior that would get you in trouble with HR is just as unacceptable here.

3. **Focus on work-related posts.**

If you're feeling the urge to share a funny meme with your colleague, make sure you post it to the right place. It's acceptable to joke around every now and then on Facebook, Twitter, and other social platforms. Bonus points if you can be both funny *and* tie it back to a relevant topic. However, be respectful of your coworkers. If you take it too far, regardless of the social platform (but especially on LinkedIn), it could still impact your reputation.

4. **Don't underestimate the importance of your photo.**

Your photo is your opportunity to make a good first impression; it's what will catch someone's attention. Even an impressive resume will be passed over if your profile picture is unprofessional or inappropriate. We came across someone with whom we have mutual connections doing Jell-O shots in their profile pic. Yes, really. We're pretty certain that's not the type of thing that fosters goodwill among prospective employers.

Although we all have a life outside of work, we want to be taken seriously by current and prospective clients and colleagues. A party animal profile photo conveys the wrong message for most audiences.

Now that you've mastered key elements of LinkedIn, let's move on to another important platform: Twitter. This network can be extremely helpful in building your brand.

Chapter 7

Becoming a Twitter Virtuoso

How to Create a Twitter Bio that Stands Out

While we love LinkedIn, we've been proponents of using Twitter for personal branding for years. Jeremy, in particular, spends a good part of every day tweeting as @jeremarketer, where he has amassed a relatively significant following. If you're looking to build your personal brand via Twitter, your bio is a great place to start.

Writing your Twitter bio may seem like a daunting task. Is it even possible to define yourself in 160 characters? Not entirely, unless you're the most boring person in the world—which we're positive is not the case. When it comes to your bio, there are some proven tactics that will help you make a powerful impact and attract more followers.

1. **Be straightforward and accurate.**

   How do you define yourself? If you browse through Twitter bios, you'll see many people go for an irreverent angle when describing themselves. You may be a Starbucks addict and have an obsession with My Little Pony, but unless those are the defining attributes of your brand, they shouldn't be emphasized in your bio. The best approach is to be direct and honest, while at the same time adding a spark of wit. People will want to follow you based on how you spend your days, and if you seem like an interesting person.

2. **Add a positive and enthusiastic spin.**

    Just like in real life, portraying yourself as upbeat and optimistic will attract more followers. Think about it: When you're meeting someone for the first time, chances are you're a little more animated and friendly in order to make a great first impression. The same principle applies on social platforms; you'll naturally draw people in if you seem exciting and engaging.

3. **Include hashtags and/or links.**

    Use keywords that will make you more likely to show up in searches, and choose your hashtags wisely to attract the right followers. If you're a dating and relationships consultant, consider using: #dating, #relationships, and #love. Also, using hashtags in your profile shows a certain degree of social media savvy. But try to find the right balance; #please #don't #overdo #it.

4. **Give people a sense of the real you.**

    There are a ridiculously high number of fake profiles out there, so make sure you present yourself in an authentic way. An easy way to do this is by adding something at the end about one of your interests—whether it's coffee, photography, or traveling—to let people see a small glimpse into who you are outside of your job. Though you do want to remain straightforward, it's also good to show connections that you're multifaceted.

How Do I Get My First 100 Followers?

Many people have trouble amassing followers on Twitter, and get discouraged too soon. As with many endeavors, you need to be a little patient. But you also need to make sure you're making the right moves. This is what you can do to get started:

1. **Run searches.**

   Simply go to Search.twitter.com or use the search function in your browser or app to find people who are interested in the same topics as you are. It's relatively easy to retweet people as an acknowledgment that you like what they're saying, but if they're busy, they won't notice that you've done so. A better tactic is to comment on their content, ask them a question, or engage with them in some way. Most people who value building connections will respond. If you write something valuable and somebody doesn't write back, they're either too swamped with comments to see yours, or they're probably not a great person to know anyway. But even if your target doesn't respond to your comments, other people commenting may notice your comment and reply.

2. **Import your address book.**

   This is an underrated tactic when starting out. What we love about importing your contacts is that you'll often find people who you want to connect to who are very relevant to your personal brand—and you just didn't know about it. Plus, you can select multiple e-mail accounts to import. Once you've done that, chances are that you will find a few contacts who signed up for Twitter and then never really did that much on the platform. You don't have to follow everybody in your address book, but you'll often find a few gems.

3. **Follow back.**

   As you follow more and more people and send out your first tweets, people will see your activity and follow you once they see you're interested in what they have to offer. Some people might try to follow you just to get you to follow them back, but if their content is interesting to you, there's no harm in doing so. And if you decide a few weeks later that they don't post content you like, you can unfollow them without much chance of them noticing.

Targeting With Twitter

Twitter may seem like an all-or-nothing communications tool, but there are actually plenty of ways to target specific demographics. Well-defined Twitter searches can also help you figure out exactly whom to have a conversation with. Use a tool such as Followerwonk to search Twitter bios and to find people who work for specific companies you're looking to do business with, and Hootsuite or Tweetdeck to segment your feeds in order to find the content and users most relevant to your brand.

With respect to Twitter, your main feed is too generalized and tough to follow. Instead, it's a good idea to break up your Twitter contacts into different segmented Twitter Lists. Using Twitter and not using Twitter Lists would be like having Force abilities but not wielding a lightsaber.

Twitter Lists

This feature has been around for years, yet is vastly underutilized by the average Twitter user. Luckily, you're not the average Twitter user. A Twitter list is simply a curated group of Twitter users that allows you to efficiently organize individual accounts in various groups and better manage your tweets. You can subscribe to a list created by another user, or, preferably, you can create your own. By creating your own list, you can easily follow the tweets of specific groups of users separate from the ones that follow you.

Lists allow you to sort your most enthusiastic followers, corporate accounts that you want to build a relationship with, people you're following but who aren't following you back, and so on, into different groups. Lists can also be used for competitive analysis: For one, you actually don't have to follow someone to place them on a list, so you can follow your competition without technically following them. On top of that, you can make a list completely private, hidden to everyone but you. These two conditions allow you to create a list, name it, say, "competitors I want to crush," and place all of your competitors' Twitter IDs on that list—all without actually following those accounts, which would give them a heads-up that you're following what they're doing.

How to Create a Twitter List

Creating a Twitter list is fairly simple. Simply go to *https://twitter.com/lists*, and then click on "create new list." You can now create a name and description for the list and specify whether it is public—in which case any user can subscribe to it—or private. After saving your list, you can add members by clicking on their profile; moreover, you do not have to be following them to add them to the list. The ways to use Twitter lists are virtually limitless, but here are a few of the most helpful ways we've found to make Twitter lists work for us:

1. **Project team directory.**

   If you're collaborating with a group of individuals on a project launch, you can find them on Twitter and gather them into a single directory. This may incentivize anyone not on Twitter to open an account, because the platform can provide a convenient way to share work-related updates and live feeds. A project directory list also allows users outside your inner circle to see all the cool people you're working with and want to be part of the fun.

2. **Event organization and management.**

   When it comes to events, Twitter lists allow participants as well as those unable to attend a means of staying updated. Using a hashtag related to the event allows anyone interested to contribute to the topic at hand, and also provides an opportunity for people to keep in touch after the event. You can add a whole bunch of people to one Twitter list using a single hashtag—which is helpful if you want to remember where you met someone.

3. **"Competitors" list.**

Creating a list comprised of potential rivals is a smart business move: It keeps you up to date with any of their new projects or endeavors, and gives you an opportunity to observe what they share on social media and the manner in which they engage with their customer base. A list of your competitors, of course, should probably be marked private as opposed to public.

4. **Extraordinary customers.**

In any line of business, a customer is of immense value and should be treated as such. Twitter lists allow you to show your gratitude to them for their loyalty. Every time you add an individual to a *public* list, they receive a notification, and this is a great way to show your appreciation to a highly valued customer. A list of exceptional customers is basically a "recognize and reward" list that will come in handy while organizing community-oriented campaigns in which you'd like to engage some of your most valued customers.

5. **Users who retweet you.**

Users who often retweet you likely share similar opinions and/or are avid fans of your brand. Just as you have a list of your favorite customers, people who frequently retweet you warrant their own list. Name this something more original than "Retweeters." Try to think of something that indicates the value they represent to you. For example, Ali has a list called "The Wind Beneath My Wings." Similarly, share from their posts what you see as potentially useful for your brand, creating a win-win situation and incentivizing them to share more of your posts.

6. **Industry players.**

   This list includes Twitter users who work in your specific field, and not just the ones you compete with for customers. Face it: You're in a dynamic, fast-paced industry. Just like you keep up with the daily news, you need to keep track of trends and updates in your field.

7. **Prospects.**

   Are you interested in striking up conversations with companies you'd like to work with? Use a social media management tool like SocialBro to search all of Twitter and find people who work at companies you're interested in, and then add them to a Prospects list. Of course, name it something less obvious—or keep it private.

One small caveat: People who don't employ lists are using too few, true, but it's also possible to create too many. Go ahead and use your account to its fullest by creating only the lists that will be most useful to you and your brand.

Interacting with People in Your Feed

Building your brand by interacting with individuals in your Twitter feed is the single-most important part of using Twitter. It shouldn't be all about posting content and updates. Broadcasting your ideas is all well and good, but if you don't make time to engage with your contacts digitally, no one is going to be there to support you when you need them. It's similar to real life: If you were the kind of person who showed up at a party and immediately started talking about yourself without much regard for what was going on with everybody else's lives, your network would become less and less inclined to listen to you.

The same principle applies, we have found, to when people post to our digital networking group, Mosaic: Members who are active and very supportive of others will get a lot of engagement when they eventually ask for a favor. On the other hand, members who only pop up when they need something tend to get very little engagement, responses, or support.

Maximizing Your Twitter Presence

One of the key ways to build up your presence is to make sure that you find the time to actually engage with people. Some professionals have actually said to us, "I'd love to have a following of 5,000 or 10,000 followers, and I'm not really doing that much on Twitter right now. What type of shortcuts can I take?" On Twitter, there is a direct correlation between the time you allocate to Twitter, the value that you add to your community, and the number of people who will follow you. To be successful, you need to make the time to engage in the first place.

Chapter 8

Networking and IRL Meetings

The Importance of IRL

Digital marketplace and e-commerce design hub Bezar launched in early 2015. It's hard for founder and CEO Bradford Shellhammer to bring himself to leave the young brand's headquarters to visit conferences and tradeshows. But Bradford compares it to the role of a politician. "I'm on the campaign trail." He has to be a brand ambassador for what the company is doing. "Being present is very important," he says.[1]

When comparing digital branding initiatives to in-person appearances, Bradford considers the latter more important. "I actually learn stuff when I'm around other cool people doing cool things," Bradford says. "It's an opportunity to be inspired. It would be foolish not to take advantage of those opportunities just because you're too busy." Plus, there's the matter of connecting with others facing the same business challenges as you are. There's a loneliness about being a CEO, managing employees, and dealing with investors, and it's nice to be around other people who are going through the same things as you are. These face-to-face experiences are what will truly build your network.

You're investing a lot of time into building your brand, so why not invest some of it into building your network? After all, your brand won't be very useful to you if nobody knows who you are. Your network is one of your most powerful assets, because it's a tool that's going to help you gain credibility from both your audience and your peers. And though we adore social networking and digital in general, it's no substitute for getting out there and meeting people face to face.

And don't lose sight of another important fact: Companies often use conferences and events to look for new talent. "It's always about the people," says John Sculley, who has headed Pepsi-Cola and Apple. "You can have super ideas and mediocre people and you won't succeed, so I always spend the most time trying to find the very best people."[2]

Nolan Bushnell, founder of Atari and Chuck E. Cheese (among many other successful tech ventures), agrees: For young entrepreneurs looking to make a name for themselves, meetups are very important. Companies such as Amazon, Google, and Apple have whole teams of people that consistently stalk meetups. So whether you're looking to find work or find talent for your own venture, you've got to have an active presence in your community's meetup ecosystem.

Bushnell has seen the importance of in-person interactions firsthand; his youngest son was just recruited by Google based on the quality of a presentation he made. An entrepreneur like his father, the younger Bushnell turned down a more-than-fair salary to stay in the startup game. If you're not attending meetups, Bushnell maintains, you're likely going to miss out on superior talent and quality opportunities.[3]

Before you begin your work on connections that you don't have, focus on the people you already know. Your peers are a great resource to help you create new connections organically, without feeling the pressure of having to meet new people immediately. By reaching out to friends, coworkers, friends, and family, you can build your network from the ground up. So this chapter is really going to help you make the most of "in real life" (IRL for short) to build your brand.

Making a Good Impression

We're talking a lot about building your brand via digital platforms, but humans are inherently social creatures. You simply can't discount the importance of building your brand IRL. This chapter is going to delve into the intricacies of truly bringing brands to life without any screens in the way—starting with first impressions.

The first seven seconds in which you meet somebody, according to science, is when you'll make a "first impression." So, whether it's for an event, a business development meeting, or any other professional setting, you have to act very quickly in order to make the proper first impression. In order to have a great meeting and be remembered in the right way—while cementing your reputation—here are some important tips:

1. **Smile!**

   Facial expressions are very important when it comes to making a good first impression. Other than Grumpy Cat, who doesn't want their personal brand to be associated with positivity? Smiling is at the start of this list for a good reason. Forty-eight percent of all Americans feel that a smile is the most memorable feature after first meeting someone.[4] And attitude and enthusiasm can be just as important as expertise and vision, so if you're excited to meet with someone, don't feel like you have to downplay that. Most of your potential contacts will appreciate that you'd leap at the chance to do something great for the company.

   Although smiling is important, you probably don't want to have a cheesy and inauthentic grin plastered across your face. Smile too widely and it's going to look like you're covering up nervousness. Or you might come across as arrogant. Even a small grin can go a long way. It says, "I'm open and approachable"—and that can make you come across as a more magnetic, attractive personality.

Not only does smiling make others feel more comfortable around you, but it also decreases the stress hormones that negatively impact your health, according to numerous studies. As the need to make a positive first impression can increase your stress level, smiling is a way to take the edge off.

2. **The right handshake.**

The handshake is accepted internationally as a professional sign of politeness. A proper handshake can convey confidence. You might be rolling your eyes at this, but the handshake is a fine art. You want to walk the line between a squeeze that comes across as incredibly tight and the dreaded limp fish. When you're meeting with people whom you trust and have known for years, ask them how they feel after shaking hands, and how your handshake feels in relation to others they've experienced.

3. **Introductions.**

You want your first seven seconds with somebody to be productive, so it's great to throw in a verbal introduction as you meet with people. Even something as simple as "fantastic to meet you" after they greet you can break the tension, and stop you from getting off into a tangent. If you have a hard time remembering names, the intro is a great place to reinforce the name of the person you just met. It doesn't have to be too involved: When your contact says, "Hi, I'm Laura," reply with a simple, "Great to meet you, Laura. I'm Geri," instead of just saying, "Hi, I'm Geri," in response.

4. **Speak clearly.**

Many people have wonderful things to say, but don't speak with any confidence. Unfortunately, that's a great way to wind up getting overlooked. You want to be able to portray yourself in a positive light and give whomever you're meeting a reason to listen to you. Don't overcorrect and get too loud, either. Studies have indicated that those who talk calmly in a deeper voice are taken more seriously.

5. **Make eye contact.**

Looking someone in the eye conveys that you are confident and interested in what they have to say. "Keep good eye contact by looking the person in the eye when he or she is communicating," advises Peter Economy, bestselling author of *Managing for Dummies*. "Keep eye contact going when you speak, because this shows you are interested in the conversation."[5] Courtney Spritzer, COO and cofounder of SOCIALFLY, agrees: "Making eye contact with someone shows that you are paying attention, and makes them feel important."[6]

Just make sure that you strike the balance. Peter warns, "Watch your eye contact, though—if you don't take breaks to contemplate your next answer, your eye contact could be viewed as staring (translation: aggressive or creepy)."

6. **Dress the part.**

If Oprah Winfrey came to a public appearance dressed in sweatpants and a T-shirt, we probably wouldn't realize how smart she is; we would get stuck on that first impression and be influenced by how she presented herself. This is true for anybody. Appearance is just about as important as body language, so make sure that you're dressed for the occasion. You don't want to skew too formal or too informal, but in case you're not sure what tone to set, it's preferable to be slightly overdressed rather than underdressed. If you're meeting with a potential client and are dressed too informally, you might give a sense that you don't really care about gaining their business.

"We live in a world where appearance matters," says Courtney Spritzer. "Dressing the part is very important. The saying 'dress for the job you want, not the job you have' is important to think about as you are deciding what to wear to the next event, job interview, or client meeting. If you look good, you tend to feel good, and it can help give you the confidence you need to network around the room."

"There's an old adage: 'Don't let the dress wear you. You wear the dress,'" says Melanie Notkin, founder of SavvyAuntie.com and author of *Otherhood*. "When I'm in a client meeting or giving a speech, I want the client or audience to be able to focus on what I'm saying, not what I'm wearing. I want to look strong, chic, and savvy. I usually wear clean, elegant lines that are not distracting and add one piece of bold jewelry to emulate strength."[7]

In today's competitive arena, entrepreneurs need to always put their best foot forward. "You are your brand, especially if you are a business owner, so making sure that your look communicates your best self is important," advises Laurel Mintz, CEO of Elevate My Brand, an L.A.–based marketing agency. Laurel advises that you maintain a signature look or color "because you are constantly marketing yourself and if there is something distinguishable, it makes you memorable."[8] For example, everyone knows Laurel is a "purple girl," so the color purple is a big part of her professional wardrobe.

"Be aware of your audience," advises Alyssa Gelbard, career advice expert.[9] Alyssa feels that younger workers often lack professionalism in how they present their brand. "It sends a message, and you can't afford that. You're sending messages without even realizing it. So if you're sitting next to someone who's worked in your industry for 15 years, you're communicating something that clashes with that standard."

7. **Body language.**

   One interesting thing about human psychology is that most of us instinctively mirror each other's body language. Think about how infectious a yawn is in a group of people. A smile between friends is contagious, too. In fact, there is a type of neuron that affects the part of the brain responsible for recognizing faces and reading facial expressions. This neuron causes the "mirroring" reaction. So when another person sees you smiling, the neuron fires and causes them to smile in response. Mirroring goes both ways; if you pick up on and reflect back the nonverbal cues of the person you're speaking with, it sends a nonverbal message that you feel what they feel. Research shows that people who experience the same emotions are likely to experience mutual trust, connection, and understanding.

   Mirroring body language is a nonverbal way of saying "we have something in common." When people say that someone gives off good energy, they're not just indulging in some New Age beliefs; they're describing mirroring and other synchronous behaviors they're not consciously aware of.

8. **Strutting your stuff.**

   You might have highly visible accessories—such as multi-colored hair, piercings, or tattoos—that you could choose to play up or down depending on your identity. If these are a core part of your identity, keep them out and wear them proudly. Just understand that not everyone is comfortable with these traditionally "unprofessional" accouterments. Jeremy is known for having a multitude of colorful iPhone cases shaped like Rilakkuma, the popular Japanese teddy bear character. Most days, he makes a point of matching his iPhone case with his outfit. He realizes that some people might not want to work with Firebrand Group because of that, but he's perfectly comfortable with people perceiving him as a bit of an eccentric. His reasoning is that, in the long term, clients who don't appreciate his creativity and whimsy won't be good fits for his business anyway. So by all means, spice things up a little bit if you deem it appropriate—just understand that not everybody will appreciate it.

As often as you can, embrace your differences and quirks. They'll help you stand out in people's minds. Albert Einstein, famous for his wild hair and somewhat-disheveled appearance, had an utter disdain of socks. In contrast, social marketing strategist Ted Rubin always wears interesting and unusual footwear[10] and regularly shares social media posts tagged #tedsockie.[11] Prominent astrophysicist Neil de-Grasse Tyson, the director of the Hayden Planetarium, is known for his colorful vests and ties. Other distinctive people—from Steve Jobs to Michael Kors to Johnny Cash—have stood out by having a personal uniform.

Physical branding isn't about having good looks; it's about having the *right* look. If you feel like something in your appearance or presentation is holding you back, try to embrace that weakness head-on and turn it into strength. If there's something about you that someone will notice, doesn't it make sense to acknowledge it and control the conversation?

In-Person Branding and Presentation

As we've noted, your brand isn't just about what you say and how you act; it's about how you represent yourself physically, too. After all, personal branding is a blend of everything that makes you who you are. Though your brand is comprised of many intangible traits, we don't want to lie to you: Your physical appearance does matter. Naturally, it's almost always the first thing that people notice about you. Your personal and professional goals, attitudes, and preferences, and how you choose to present yourself all combine to form your brand.

Choosing clothing consistent with your brand will often help sell your story, and projecting the image of success (even before you're fully able to attain it) can give you a confidence boost that will make it easier for you to achieve your goals. The popular TLC reality show *What Not to Wear* was a great resource for those interested in thinking about their physical presentation. Hosts Stacy London and Clinton Kelly might not have considered themselves personal branding experts, per se, but they helped participants express the qualities they were looking to embody simply by updating their wardrobes.

Stacy and Clinton began each episode by interviewing participants to get a sense of their hobbies, lifestyle, and personal preferences. For example: Were they creative? Were they active or sedentary? Were they parents? What type of career were they in? The hosts then spoke to the participant's friend and family to get their perspective. This is similar to the process we're advocating for in this book. We've already started by asking you to define your brand, and in Chapter 13 we'll give you advice for requesting feedback from friends and colleagues.

In every episode, the big makeover reveal was a truly satisfying moment for both the viewers and the participants. Not only that, but the participants started feeling better as well. It's clear they felt more confident, which led to an improvement in overall happiness and usually greater success in turn. You might not have the benefit of a reality show, but you can still take your physical presentation more seriously and take pride in it.

Networking and Conferences

When people are thinking of their physical presentation, it goes beyond clothes; they might even start to think about their skin. When beauty entrepreneur Sarah Kugelman was overworked and overstressed a number of years ago, it took a toll on her complexion. Her journey to wellness helped her find more than health and happiness; her personal experiences and dedication to teaching others about managing stress became the inspiration for Skyn Iceland, an award-winning skincare line designed to soothe stressed-out complexions. As she discovered, it's the in-person interactions with customers and fellow entrepreneurs that have really helped grow her business.

No matter where she goes or whom she talks to, everyone has their own story about how stress has affected their life and their health. "It's the in-person piece that creates a dialogue," says Sarah. "I can inform and teach and advise, which helps spread the word, but then it also inspires me back. It's this self-perpetuating cycle that I find so powerful."[12]

Sarah attends a large number of conferences yearly, and tailors her approach to every event. For each event, she has a good reason for going and knows what she wants to get out of attending. In her eyes, if you don't think about your objectives in advance, you won't get the most out of your time investment. "Earlier in my career I would go to an event without a plan, and then afterwards I would think, 'I should have talked to that person,' or, 'I have this business idea, I should have looked for somebody who could help me with that,'" she says. So now Sarah puts together a plan well in advance, looks up speakers and fellow attendees, and makes a mental check-list of what she wants to accomplish while she's there.

In addition, Sarah has a formula for determining how often she speaks at conferences versus how often she simply attends to learn and network. "Speaking builds your credibility as a businessperson and an industry expert. It's a great way to further your networking," she says. But just be aware that speaking can hinder your ability to experience everything at the event because you'll be so focused on your talk. Meeting with people one-on-one can be as useful, if not more useful, than speaking to an audience. Sarah recommends a 50/50 split for speaking and attending.

If you want to speak at a conference, there are a number of approaches. If you haven't spoken before, look for calls for speakers. Finding these can be as simple as Googling the phrase "call for speakers" along with a particular city or industry. If people like what you have to say in your first outing, both organizers and attendees will remember you and be open to your speaking at future events. Just think about how you're going to stand out when you're planning what you're going to talk about. Sarah recalls, "When we went to the WWD Digital Beauty Conference, we did our presentation from the perspective of a smaller, independent brand. And it turned out to be great, because no one else took that angle." Try to find the topic that's a little bit off the beaten path. You want to offer something that nobody else at that conference is going to bring to the table.

Gaby Dalkin of *What's Gaby Cooking*, whom we met earlier, has this advice for others looking to get into her field: "Networking is huge. I went to so many different food conferences and blogging events, especially when I was starting out."[13] A point of differentiation is key as well. Like Sarah, Gaby advocates for having a unique point of view. "Figure out what it is that you want to stick to and stay really true to that. I think that's going to take you a long way," she says.

Adam Cohen of *DaDa Rocks* certainly stands out: In a sea of mom bloggers, he was one of the first dad bloggers on the block. When Adam went to BlogHer and other top mom blog conferences, he was determined to meet everyone he could, including brand representatives and PR people. What was the result? New York's mom bloggers took Adam under their wings.

One of the first steps Adam took was to meet representatives from all his favorite baby companies to find out about new product launches, and better position himself to test products and give exclusive reviews. "That was my goal when I went to the ADC [the biggest baby gear show in America]."[14] He found that his pro-fatherhood, down-to-earth nature really resonated with the brands, as it was something that they really hadn't seen much of in that space. These conferences were one of the most crucial factors in Adam's networking, the expansion of his brand, and ultimately his success.

Sure, it's always a good idea to meet up with people in your industry. But how do you know who's going to attend a specific event? One digital tool we use to see who will be where is Lanyrd. Known as "the social conference directory," Lanyrd is a crowdsourced platform owned by Eventbrite. Users can sign in with their Twitter or LinkedIn account and receive event suggestions. For example, when Ali logs in, she receives recommendations pertaining to writing, strength training, and cooking. After receiving recommendations, a user can hit "attend" or "track." The former signifies that he or she will be at the event—so everyone in their network can take note—whereas the latter is essentially bookmarking an event so you can research it later.

Convincing Your Boss to Send You to a Conference

Before you approach your boss to present a new idea, you've got to be prepared, be confident, and have sufficient knowledge of the matter you want to discuss. And if you want approval to attend a conference, you'll probably need to build a strong case. Be ready to explain what makes this particular event unique and worthwhile.

Here are three key reasons to attend a conference:

1. You will learn the latest, most forward-thinking strategies. Industry leaders are always ahead of the curve. In order to stay competitive, you must also be knowledgeable about current trends and successful tactics. It's in your best interest—as well as your boss's—to take advantage of what these leading experts have to say. Learning from the best will put you ahead of the pack.

2. You will know where to focus your time and energy to see results. Many companies waste time running test campaigns and going through a lot of trial and error before discovering the formula to success. In fact, inefficiencies may cost a given company as much as 20 to 30 percent. A good conference will include speakers who will not only challenge your current way of thinking, but will share actionable advice.

3. This is a networking opportunity you can't pass up. Some of the world's top experts in your field will be there, and

you will have access to the best and brightest thought leaders in the industry. In as little as five minutes, you can learn a lot. And who knows, maybe you'll even create a few new partnerships!

While you're having a discussion about getting approval, keep a few techniques in mind. First, pick the right time. In order to make sure you have your boss's undivided attention, you should plan to speak during a time of day that is as stress-free as possible for both of you. For example, don't try to schedule time on a day where it's 2 p.m. and your supervisor hasn't had lunch yet. You probably won't get an approval from someone who is hangry (hunger-induced anger).

Next, create a strong, succinct proposal. This will not only help keep your thoughts organized, but might also impress your boss—a good pitch demonstrates that you've done your homework, done your prep work, and are taking this opportunity seriously. Don't make it longer than it has to be. Trim the fat and make it relevant to the questions you anticipate from your supervisor.

Always, always be enthusiastic. Passion and energy can be contagious. If you go into the meeting with confidence and enthusiasm, your boss will be more inclined to comply and give you what you're asking for. Even if you're nervous, channel those nerves into excitement and it will make you come across in a positive light.

Of course, every boss is different, and it pays to listen to your gut. For the most part, however, if you follow these guidelines, you will make it much easier for your boss to say yes. And, wherever you're going, hopefully we'll see you there.

Face-to-Face Meetings

Conferences and events are important to growing your network and raising your visibility, but smaller face-to-face meetings can be just as valuable. They might not seem like the ideal way to reach a broad audience, but you don't just want your relationships to have breadth; you also want them to have depth. Though digital socialization is necessary to up your numbers, in-person conversations are just as meaningful. Sometimes they're even more significant. Digital media increases brand awareness; real-life interactions create loyalty.

The benefits of branching out are immense. By getting out into the world and exposing yourself to challenging ideas, you are better off for the experience. It exposes you to new modes of thinking and forces you to become more flexible. Whom you spend your time with is almost as important as what you spend your time on, and you should always seek relationships with others who complement your personality. In the life of a busy entrepreneur, finding the right friends can require a concerted effort, but it is worth it in the long run. Finding likeminded people who mesh with you is key, and you will benefit greatly from working with those who have a history of positive collaborative endeavors and a willingness to give back.

Sarah Kugelman considers these encounters to be indispensable. "I feel like you just can't do things on e-mail and phone the way you can do things in person. I've never gotten a big new account [to carry Skyn Iceland] without meeting in person," she says. Just keep in mind that there's a lot that leads up to a successful in-person meeting. It's very rare that you'll just get on the phone with a contact and say, "I want to come talk to you," and—BOOM—meeting. "I'll go through a bazillion e-mails and phone calls," Sarah confides, "but it's the meeting that's the transition point."

Most people you meet face to face will encounter your digital persona first, so it's important that the way you talk about yourself is consistent. "This is one of the biggest discrepancies people struggle with: If you're great on paper, but you talk about yourself in a different way when you're communicating with someone in person, you're shooting yourself in the foot," advises Alyssa Gelbard, the career expert we met earlier. "There is nothing more frustrating than being excited about bringing someone in to talk to them, and then they're talking about themselves in a completely different way and you're thinking to yourself, 'Where's the person with the insightful tweets? That's who I wanted to talk to. Who's *this* guy?'"

Of course, if you're nervous about meeting someone (or a group of people) in person, it's hard to relax and be yourself. You want to make a good impression, right? Right, but you probably don't need to try that hard. That's why we recommend simply trying to relate to people on a personal level. That's the secret of expert conversationalists: Find a way to connect to a new contact in a way that seems natural, not forced. The goal during any first encounter is to appear inviting and personable.

Once you've successfully grabbed someone's attention, the next—and more challenging—step is to keep it. So be direct, yet sincere. Get to the point as quickly as possible, and keep it simple. If you tend to freeze or babble when you're nervous, it may help you to prepare some questions in advance for the person you're meeting with. Remember, you wouldn't want someone to talk your ear off, so always be mindful of the other person's time. Keep it simple, be prepared, and keep it short!

"The challenge is to break through and ensure they view you as a colleague—someone 'like them'—rather than a stranger impinging on their time," says Dorie Clark, marketing strategist and teacher at Duke's Fuqua School of Business.[15] As you don't want to appear too aggressive or overeager, a first meeting shouldn't be longer than 20 or 30 minutes. Starting small lets your connection know that you respect their time, and if you request a quick chat it will probably increase your chances of landing the meeting.

One more thing to keep in mind is you don't necessarily have to set up an event or meeting in order to interact with your audience or clients in person. Check out panel discussions, meet-ups, and presentations that are relevant to your brand. These allow you to build connections with your audience and peers, as well as learn from others in your field. If you're planning to attend a conference or workshop, do a little research; there are often tweet-ups and hashtags created for these occasions. These give you added visibility and make it easy for people to reply to you or retweet that clever insight you just had. Ideally, you should be promoting your digital channels when face-to-face with your audience. Connecting these two relationships creates an association that will last long after the actual event has

ended, and can really boost your social presence. We call this the
virtuous circle.

Maximize Your Time

Given how crucial meetings can be, we've compiled some tips
or strategies that you can use to make sure you're getting the most
out of your time with a connection. First of all: Always be prepared.
Make sure your presentation is geared toward your audience. Know
who they are and what they're looking for.

Sarah Kugelman likes to strategize and have her presentation
ready well before a meeting. That way she doesn't feel like she's
scrambling or trying to figure things out at the last minute. She also
pays close attention to the meeting's agenda and hammers out the
details in advance—everything from how long she'll have to meet to
where it's going to be held, who's attending, and everyone's goals or
objectives.

Most importantly, Sarah asks herself, "What's my 'show and
tell' that will get people excited?" There always has to be some kind
of sizzle aspect to your meeting. She once had a conversation with
someone who wanted to form a business alliance, but their presentation was so dry and boring that she couldn't wait to get off the
phone. "I never want anybody to feel like that in a meeting with me.
I want them to be inspired about what I'm talking about. I only feel
like I've done my job if I leave the meeting and people are excited
and energized."

If you've had a successful meeting, you'll know it; you won't be
able to stop firing off ideas. It's a little like dating. There should be
chemistry. You should hope that you're going to get a "second date."
And to get there, you need to put your best foot forward.

Being Uncomfortable

Working with other people is an incredibly useful way to network. But getting to know new people also forces you to work outside your comfort zone. Jeremy is very sociable, and by now we're

both practiced and comfortable talking to people. But though Ali realizes the importance of making connecting with others look like second nature, she's not quite as outgoing. And we've realized that many of our successful, self-assured colleagues have struggled with this, too. The important thing to know about poise is that you often can't tell who really has it and who's trying the "fake it 'til you make it" approach.

"I was so painfully shy. And it's taken so much work to overcome it," shares Sarah Kugelman. "I thought for many years I was going to be an actress. So I used to play a part. I'd pretend I was a confident, knowledgeable businesswoman to get me through a meeting or presentation." At Sarah's first job out of business school, she attended big meetings where the upper-level execs would ask questions of the most junior people in the room. She couldn't figure out how everyone knew all the answers—until one day somebody asked a question that she actually knew the answer to. But the junior associate didn't give the right response. They just faked it. And that's when Sarah realized that maybe people had been faking it the whole time.

Feeling shy or awkward is one of the major problems entrepreneurs deal with early on in their career. But if you're letting that stop you from attending a conference or scheduling a meeting, just remember that you're not the only one who feels that way. Cofounder and COO of SOCIALFLY Courtney Spritzer shares, "We have built our business on networking, but oftentimes it can be intimidating to enter a room filled with strangers."

It can be helpful to have a friend or partner to go to events and meetings with if you're nervous about attending alone, but don't let that get in the way of connecting with new people. Usually the first few encounters are the most nerve-wracking, so instead of sticking by the side of the person you know, come up with a strategy in advance. That will help you feel more prepared, and lessen the in-person jitters. What's Courtney's secret? "I always give myself the goal of talking to two to three people before leaving." Once you're over that initial barrier of talking to the first unfamiliar person, you'll feel more comfortable. You might even surprise yourself and end up staying longer—and making more connections—than you originally anticipated.

Aim High

Don't just focus on your peers. Getting to know experts in your field is worth the time and effort. But it doesn't happen overnight. You never know who you'll meet or how they'll help you days, weeks, or even months later.

Sarah Kugelman had met an industry leader who seemed really interested in working with her, but after an initial meeting she didn't hear back from him, so she thought he didn't like her brand. About a year later, he called her about a new business opportunity and ever since, he's been one of the most helpful and encouraging people in her career. The lack of response wasn't about Sarah—her contact was just busy and trying to figure out what his next step was. At the time there wasn't anything that her brand was right for, but when the time came, his synapses fired and he called her up. You never know where that opportunity is going to come from.

As you connect with more experts, they can provide advice, and some may even become regular contacts. The connections you build in your field will help you find mentors and discover what it takes to succeed in establishing your brand. They can share tips, connections, and other intangibles that help you to develop both as a brand and as a person.

Build Your Circles

Anuj Desai is a man who not only knows how to network—he loves it. One of the rising stars in the rapidly growing field of health-care information technology, Anuj has networked his way into a leadership position at major companies and won several prestigious awards for his accomplishments.

Anuj serves as director of business development for the New York eHealth Collaborative, where he's been one of the key forces behind the development of the Statewide Health Information Network of

New York (SHIN-NY), which is essentially a secure information network that allows healthcare providers the ability to share patient records across the state.

Streamlining information and stripping away inefficient communication is a major part of Anuj's company's goals, and his career is centered on improving the flow of information. In fact, some might find it ironic that Anuj's job relies on the arguably inefficient task of peer-to-peer, face-to-face networking. But although virtual interconnectedness is Anuj's bread and butter, he recognizes how much new relationships are worth, and holds great stock in his ability to make those connections.

Anuj's brand centers around not only having the ability, but also the drive to develop those relationships. "I want to constantly find new connections," he says. "And you don't know where they're going to be or where they're going to go. I encourage folks trying to build their brand not just to look within their own business circle, but to go to nontraditional places to find others, anything from tech meet-ups to Renaissance Weekends."[16] These interactions can develop into extremely beneficial relationships. It might not be right away, A to B, but down the road you will start to see dividends.

ROR (Return on Relationships)

Part of what has made Anuj successful is being open to helping others with no immediate return in sight. "There are a lot of new players" coming in to the field, he says. "They're all looking for guidance in what to do in healthcare IT, so I like being that person."

Forming real relationships with both clients and employers allows them to see you as a person, and have respect for your own personal goals. Kindness or friendship such as what Anuj exhibits can pay off—and sometimes it does so in unexpected and significant ways.

In fact, a personal relationship landed Anuj on *Crain's* Top 40 Under 40 list. He had formed a good relationship with the editor in chief, and talked to her about what his firm was doing. "And she actually asked me to nominate people for the list, and after I did, she asked, 'What about you?' She asked me to put a bio together, and I submitted on the very last day. Three weeks later she e-mailed me and said I got it."

Anuj's efforts have also won the support and respect of his CEO, which allows him to do his job and work on his personal brand simultaneously. But that kind of loyalty and trust is earned with time. "[My CEO] lets me take risks, go to nonconventional conferences, and speak at different events, because he knows that a lot of the relationships we've had as an organization were found and forged by me, and finding those connections that develop into something else," Anuj shares.

That sort of freedom and trust helps immensely to use your position to further your personal brand. Not only has Anuj's work furthered the companies he has worked for, it has also displayed his competency in a very public way and potentially opens doors for him down the line. "I'm now speaking on panels at conferences," says Anuj. "I realize that my brand has an influence in how successful I can be in my job, and how successful my organization can be."

Use Your Momentum

Anuj benefited greatly from being on the *Crain's* Top 40 Under 40 list: "If I compare my personal career before and after *Crain's*, it was a launch pad. It got so much attention on so many different levels, because people follow these lists like you would not believe. After *Crain's* I got two other big awards, and I think those were because of *Crain's*! So it really builds on itself."

The importance of trust and relatability cannot be understated. In fact, Anuj emphasized that his major goal at conferences—even conferences where he is a speaker—is to meet people. "When I go, I'm usually out there trying to meet people and network. A successful conference is not about content; it's about good people I met who I can follow up with to make relationships." Anuj does speak at conferences quite a bit, but besides his own session, he'll attend a few more at most, and spend the rest of the time meeting new people.

Anuj has chosen to center his life around the spread of information, from his work to his personal ambitions. Though he may work in information technology, he has made it clear that sometimes the best thing to do is close the laptop and get out there, to meet people face to face, and cultivate relationships in person. Again, networking and building your brand is not just about breadth; it's about depth. Establishing trust is a very important part of human nature, and to do so in a more personal manner appeals to people on a much deeper level than only connecting through digital channels.

Starting Over in a New Location

Your network can help you in ways you don't even realize, and the work we're having you do won't just benefit your career. Defining your brand and working on your interpersonal skills has a number of real-life applications. As we mentioned earlier, in 2014, Ali moved from her longtime home of New York to Philadelphia. Although she's enjoying her new city, there have been some ups and downs as she got to know the landscape and make connections. Relocating is almost always stressful. You have to acclimate to a new town and adjust to not having immediate access to your usual social and professional connections. However, doing some prep work before moving day can help you make a smooth transition.

Your personal and work-related contacts probably aren't coming with you, right? Maybe not physically, but the odds are pretty good that you know someone who knows someone in your new location. Ali already knew a couple of people in Philly, but when she asked friends and colleagues if they had any connections, she was surprised how many names and e-mail addresses she received. Try looking up old acquaintances and former coworkers; you never know who has a friend, relative, or old business partner you could chat with. Getting together for coffee or a drink will help you explore your new stomping grounds, too.

While you're meeting new people, don't overlook professional associations. Do you already belong to a group in your field or industry? See if there's a local chapter. If not, start one! Unless you're in an extremely remote location, it's likely that there are people with similar interests who would love to connect with their peers. You might get tired of cheese plates after a few events, but you won't ever stop appreciating the different people you meet or the potential opportunities for career building.

Forming relationships and making friends and allies among your colleagues is crucial in order to build a foundation of support and growth. But you need more than that in order to get the most out of your brand. On top of that, you need to crowdsource your support. By reaching out to a larger audience, you will find that the collective support and input you gain from a larger group can be even more beneficial than that of your closest friends.

Chapter 9

Authenticity

Is Being Authentic Important?

In the last chapter, we talked about making connections IRL. When's the last time you met someone at a conference or some other event, found them to be overwhelmingly inauthentic, and went out of your way to stay in touch with them? So, to cut to the chase: Yes, it's incredibly important to be authentic. The term "personal branding" sounds like the creation of an alter ego, which is something that many people—understandably—shy away from. But that's a misconception; personal branding isn't about creating a new persona. Your personal brand is the condensed version of your core values and interests. You-Concentrate. People are complex and varied, and personalities cannot be easily described in the shorthand that companies use. In order to stand out, we need unifying ideas that our audiences can easily remember. It's far too easy to blend in with the thousands of other people creating content.

Many people distrust the term "personal branding." They prefer "reputation" or other similar words to describe people. Such labels sound more human and less corporate. But we believe that the function of a personal brand is to be just that: business-oriented. You don't create a personal brand in order to make friends; you create a personal brand to achieve a certain objective. Your ultimate goal is to condense the most relevant parts of your personality (and your reputation) into an idea that reaches people. This becomes extremely important when you want your name and your brand to spread and become recognizable.

People dislike using the same method of referring to companies to refer to people. But nobody talks about how, "that one Website where you can connect with friends is great," and they don't laud "the little birdy Website thing where people can post small messages." Instead, they refer directly to Facebook or Twitter. These are solid, identifiable entities, and that is what people are striving to become when they create personal brands. If you're branding yourself, you have to think about all of the different facets that go into your presentation. This includes everything from your professional headshot and the quality and scope of your online portfolio to the size of your online presence. Establishing a presence even encompasses indications of your core brand qualities, such as humor or honesty.

When it comes to branding, just using the word "authentic" can be kind of a detached signifier—something that you might be tempted to use to catch your public's eye. Don't succumb to the temptation to use authenticity as a device. You want to genuinely signify high quality and reliability. You want your brand to be the modern equivalent of a maker's mark, a symbol of something of value and of use. Your brand doesn't mean anything if you don't stand behind it. If what your brand represents is empty, you have to look at how you're using "authentic" and make sure that you're showing your authenticity, not just telling people that you are authentic. Authenticity can also be signaled in subtle ways, not just proclaimed loudly.

Authenticity: Can It Live Alongside Self-Promotion?

Most people associate "personal brand" with being phony or calculated. But personal branding should be something you see as positive and powerful. It can be incredibly useful to you in the context of your profession, not to mention your livelihood. Part of your brand is the perception of who you are, and what you're trying to communicate. This is where authenticity enters the conversation.

Think of it this way: You probably couldn't find many reasonable professionals who would say, "You should be 100 percent authentic 100 percent of the time. When you go into a job interview, if you like to wear sandals and superhero-themed T-shirts, why on Earth would you wear a suit and tie?" Everybody acknowledges that if you're in a position where you want to be perceived well, and where people are evaluating you, it's acceptable and even favorable to dress up. It's normal to want to present yourself in the best possible light. At the same time, there's a mentality that to truly be yourself in some professional avenues, such as social media, you need to be yourself and put everything out there, be it good or bad.

The best approach is the truth, which lies somewhere in the middle. It makes sense to bring a degree of deliberation to the content you put out into the world. For example, look at your engagement on Facebook. Do you share posts that encompass both the highs and lows of your daily existence, or do you mention achievements and interactions that portray you at your best? Most people share stories that help them appear to be who they want to be, and how they hope others will see them, whether that's funnier, more successful, a more frequent exerciser, and so forth.

Everyone engages in curation, but not everyone does it well. It takes a certain media acumen, an understanding of the unwritten social contract between the consumer of content and said content's creator. Many people are actively trying to self-promote and build their personal brand, but the act of putting yourself out there has to be done skillfully, or it can actually become detrimental. Something as simple as posting a picture to your Instagram feed can actually be a subtle, nuanced choice. Online audiences are hypersensitive to any overt positioning that makes someone seem inauthentic.

Are these social identities we construct idealized versions of ourselves? Yes, but that doesn't make them untrue. Instead of asking if something is phony or real, self-promotional or authentic, we think the real question should be couched in terms of whether it lends value or not. Are you enriching your brand? Are you adding to the conversation? Or are you performing the equivalent of patting yourself on the back, to no particular end, and possibly to your detriment?

One person who deals with the balance between authenticity and self-promotion is relationship expert and author Andrea Syrtash. She's someone who does quite a few live appearances. In fact, Andrea has spoken everywhere from conferences to spas to the flagship Lord & Taylor in Manhattan. She feels that being accessible is a key factor when you're building your brand. People want to feel like they can talk to you—that you're willing to listen to their input and what they need.

"Nothing is too small for me, especially when I was starting out," shares Andrea.[1] When she was hosting a show at 30 Rockefeller Plaza, she would still occasionally go from there to an interview with a blogger who might have an audience of 10 people. "Sometimes you build loyalty through the smaller outlets, the smaller networks."

Many people feel uncomfortable at the prospect of self-promoting. We're taught from a very young age to be modest and to shy away from talking ourselves up, but that mentality can be harmful as you work on your brand. It's important to recognize the difference between self-promoting and self-aggrandizing. You're not being a braggart when you spread your message; you're demonstrating what you can do for your audience.

"I didn't go into this thinking I was building a brand," says Andrea. "I only started to become conscious of how I was shaping my brand three or four years in."

A writer at heart, it was only within the last few years that Andrea really cared about monetizing her brand. For her, the reward was to put good advice out there, as she saw lots of BS advice in the marketplace. "I don't think anything is more important than relationships," says Andrea. Developing her brand is what allows her to reach the widest range of people who could benefit from her advice.

For another good example of how to be your best, most authentic self, take a cue from lifelong athlete Claudia Lebenthal, who built an impressive career in publishing at Condé Nast as the creative and photo director at *Women's Sports & Fitness*. After cowriting a book called *Stoked: The Evolution of Action Sports*, she founded StyleofSport.com, which celebrates the intersection of sports with fashion, design, art, and culture. The Website is a fusion of Claudia's passion and expertise, which is why she's a big advocate of using your real life, physical presence to reinforce your brand. "It has to have a really personal feel to it. No matter how big we get, I want Style of Sport to retain its identity. Not missing a beat, never missing a detail, loving your reader, loving your audience…that's what it's all about," she says.[2]

The Risks of Being Inauthentic

Personal brands *are* a constructed entity, but that's okay. It doesn't mean they're fake. You can highlight certain parts of your personality or character in order to present a solid image; that doesn't make them less true. The only bad application would be to try to be something you're not, which is something to avoid anyway. Not only is this unethical, but it could backfire on you in a major way once people find out the truth.

Be careful how you present yourself if you can't stand behind your persona. As a culture, we've become obsessed with the origins of what we consume, from media to food and drink. Celebrities are either criticized for being "fake" or revered for being "real." The truth, however, is somewhere in the middle: Most famous people have an image that is (to some degree) manufactured. From Tiger

Woods to George Takei to Robert Downey Jr., you're looking at manufacturing on some level or another.

You want to brand yourself in a way that appeals to a lot of people. Your brand is your reputation, and the foundation of your business or personal career. But many people, trying to put forth their best selves, make the mistake of engaging in deceptive behaviors. This is a risky and inadvisable approach. If you manipulate and mislead others or try to pander to an audience that doesn't fit with who you are, you risk being called out. This can end up hurting your image beyond the scope of that one issue.

Simulating authenticity can backfire in a big way. Look at the backlash against "healthy" brands Naked Juice and Odwalla. These fresh, natural drink companies are actually part of the industrial conglomerates PepsiCo. and Coca-Cola, respectively, and when this fact came to light, health-conscious consumers reacted with displeasure, to say the least. PepsiCo. doled out more than $9 million in settlements after becoming embroiled in a class action lawsuit over use of phrases such as: "100% Juice," "100% Fruit," "non-GMO," and "All Natural," among others. There was a perception of inauthenticity, and the corporate brand took a hit. The same principle applies when we're thinking about our personal brands.

It's difficult to get away with inauthenticity for long. The experiences that people have with you—whether direct or indirect—shape their perceptions and their expectations. If you consistently fail to align yourself with the image you're trying to portray, then sooner or later your audience will catch on. Deception might pay some dividends in the short term, but eventually you will find yourself stuck because you didn't develop the skills, character, and work ethic necessary to advance legitimately. It's possible to be authentic while still building an engaging narrative. Look at your unique abilities and the value that only you can offer. Highlight qualities that you actually possess and are proud of.

Claudia Lebenthal of Style of Sport never intended to become known as a resource, but soon realized that many people see her that way. "I am the Style of Sport brand, so I'm representing the site all the time. I'm conscious about what I put on to wear to work. I ask myself, 'Is this the Style of Sport sort of look?'" In fact, Claudia believes that her embodiment of the Style of Sport ethos is the key to her success. "I don't even think I could do a Website about sport and fashion unless I was into sports and had a certain style. I have to have both those qualities; otherwise I'm kind of bullshitting people. Being known as someone who does these sports and loves the gear is my biggest selling point. I think when you are the brand, you've got to be the brand 24/7."

Authenticity vs. Storytelling

Many people want to present an idealized version of their life to the world. Though authenticity is important, the idea of storytelling is key to a compelling personal brand. In order to be an effective storyteller, what do you share and what do you keep private? Is everything supposed to be public at this point? Some of these are questions only you can answer. Some people choose to share (or bare) it all; others keep their personal relationships private, but are more open about their work. It will largely depend on your personality and your industry.

Although Claudia lives and breathes her brand down to the smallest detail, she admits that there is room for variation at Style of Sport, even if it's something she wouldn't personally own or wear. "If it's all only me, it could get a little too narrow," she acknowledges. In order to engage your audience, you have to broaden your range. "I look at it like this: If my lifestyle was a certain way, would I wear these things or use this gear? Would the woman going to spinning at 7:30 a.m. wear that?" Claudia makes sure to consider who the reader is while still staying true to the essence of her brand.

Have you ever had a chance to observe a friend or family member when they didn't know that anybody was paying attention to them? People often think that the best way of seeing the true version of somebody is to watch what they do when they think nobody's looking. Similarly, when people are considering doing business with a company, they don't just look at the business's Website to get a sense of whether or not they are a good fit; they also check out the owner. Some of the places that prospects will look include your LinkedIn, Twitter, Facebook, blogs, guest articles that you've written, and places in which you've been quoted. If you run a small business, it's very important to build up your personal brand in order to build trust with potential customers. If they like what they see after investigating, chances are that your reputation will have a positive impact on your business, and your chances of acquiring more customers.

Though your brand can precede you in a positive way, there are also drawbacks to having a strong online presence. If there's a YouTube video of you from college doing shots off of the bartender's stomach, that's probably not the image that you want to project. As you're removing everything that's objectionable, try to seed the Internet with mentions of yourself that establish you as a positive influence who is very knowledgeable in your field. You want to come across as helpful and authentic, and a thought leader in the area in which you want to be known as a subject matter expert. There are a lot of small business owners who stay small because they think small. They don't realize that they might truly be a thought leader in one particular niche. If you have the ability to elevate yourself to a position of authority within your industry, why not take advantage of it? People are looking to hire authorities.

Your brand means a lot, or it should. It's more than just your logo, your name, or your catchphrase. It needs to embody your personality, energy, attitude, character, and values. Your brand is a reflection of who you are. It's a reflection of what you believe in, what you offer, and your driving purpose. Your brand is an argument for why people should pay attention to you.

A deeper brand needs to have a deeper connection with its audience. A few Facebook fans and Twitter followers do not make a loyal audience. You need to establish a more intimate relationship with your audience, and that starts with engagement. This is where authenticity comes into play. You really, *really* can't fake this stuff. If you don't really and truly believe in your brand, if you don't support it with everything you've got, then nobody is going to be convinced to join you.

How to Be Authentic

"Just be yourself" is one of the most clichéd pieces of advice. We won't tell you to just be yourself, but we will tell you this: *Don't be anybody else.* Comparing yourself to others in your field is common and is even a good way of seeing what your peers are doing, but make sure your actions align with your personal branding statement. You're allowed to use others for reference, as long as you don't pick one to copy. Or reevaluate your statement.

Part of establishing a strong personal brand is having confidence around it. If you don't believe in the story that you're telling, how can you expect anybody else to? At some point, a PhD candidate goes from a candidate studying for a degree to a vetted PhD in their particular realm of study. The same thing is true if you're going from the planning stages of a particular strategy to actually doing it, even if there's not a particular degree involved. Now, it would be one thing if self-doubt could be of use to you in pursuing success, but that's not the case. We aren't saying to not have any self-doubt; a healthy amount of it will often make an individual think things through and reflect upon their strategies. If you keep thinking about whether or not you can make it, and if you keep on being worried that everybody is going to laugh at what you want your brand to stand for, chances are you have too much self-doubt. Don't let it become a distraction that slows you down and impedes your chances for success. After all, unless you're telling outright lies or being highly disingenuous, the people that you encounter are, for the most part, not looking to poke holes in your story.

By consistently proving that your brand reflects your values and principles, you can build trust in and loyalty to your brand. If you feel genuine belief and excitement about the person you are and the work you're doing, that will become obvious to those around you, and it will interest and attract others.

Chapter 10

Juggling Personal Brand Identity

Embracing Multiple Facets of Oneself

Bradford Shellhammer of Bezar feels lucky he's chosen a profession where, if he separated out his professional and personal brands, it would be to his detriment. His personal and professional brands "reinforce each other and feed off of one another."[1] However, many professionals aren't as lucky as Bradford. In fact, many experience a bit of a challenge in balancing multiple aspects of their brand.

Take Jason Miller of LinkedIn, for example. Jason takes his day job seriously, but he's also serious about his fun. Outside of his 9 to 5 at LinkedIn, he's a diehard concertgoer and music aficionado—and that interest has helped him stand out professionally. After working at Sony for 12 years, Jason decided to transition from the music industry into tech marketing. He felt like he had to reinvent himself professionally and went back to school to take classes in digital marketing. At the same time, he drew inspiration from Ann Handley and C.C. Chapman's content marketing bible, *Content Rules*, which emphasizes the importance of injecting your personality into everything you do. But the conversation around B2B marketing was led by people who had been in the industry forever, and it felt faceless and impersonal to Jason. Going from rock 'n' roll to B2B was a culture shock as well as a shift in essential skills. But the Marketo team liked Jason's attitude enough to give him a chance, and his articles about music intrigued them.

We all have different sides to us, both personally and professionally. There's the shipping and logistics coordinator who does stand-up comedy on the side, the strategy consultant who's also a stay-at-home dad, or the 55-year-old photographer who, until two years ago, had worked as an actuary for three decades. Being multifaceted is part of what makes us human.

As a result, sometimes we feel like we have to juggle identities. We call trying to balance too many identities *personal brand overload*. Obviously, keeping track of many different identities isn't easy, but many of us feel like we have to be everything to everyone. However, the most successful brands are those who know their identity, know who their customers are, and know how they can fulfill a very specific need in their customers' lives.

You need to figure out what it is that you're good at, what you want to do, and what you want to be known for. Market those aspects of your brand, and really own that idea of what you are. The best way to achieve that is to start to unite how different people perceive you into one harmonious whole. This often involves reintroducing yourself—literally and/or figuratively—to individuals who are important to your success. This can include clients, partners, prospective employers, colleagues at your company, industry contacts—you get the idea.

Reconciling Personal Brand and Corporate Brand

When Jason Miller was transitioning into the B2B world, he quickly realized that B2B marketing didn't have to be dry—although it often was. He started using music analogies and talking about his love for heavy metal in his work. Jason found that if you have a strong personality, if you can use humor effectively, and if you can draw compelling comparisons, you can help people learn and remember your content. Jason notes, "Your average reader won't remember '5 reasons you need to go digital,' but they will remember '5 content management lessons I learned from Spinal Tap.'"[2] And when someone in the industry told Jason that "social marketing doesn't work for B2B," he was more than happy to prove them wrong.

Jason's love of music and marketing helped him find a way to stand out effectively. Instead of shying away from what other people might worry would come across as an inconsistency, he used his passion for music to help his audience—and prospective employers—see him as a well-rounded and interesting individual. When he came to work for LinkedIn, he was able to find a nice balance between the professional and the personal by using his knack for creating content that's both informative and compelling. "I'm kind of an entertainer stuck in a B2B marketer's body," Jason jokes. "I'm into music, and I'm really into comedy. So if you take Guns N' Roses and Black Sabbath, some humor, and cross those with B2B marketing, you come up with something that's unique, funny, memorable, and actually useful. I try to infuse every keynote presentation with that mix."

Of course, not everyone responds 100 percent positively to Jason's distinctive mix of Motley Crüe, humor, and marketing. But you can't please everyone all the time, nor should you try. Jason works hard to make every presentation valuable to the audience; every comedy bit and story is anchored by solid information. And sometimes accidents happen in the moment, like when he accidentally dropped the mic (literally, not metaphorically) and then automatically dropped an F-bomb. One of the pieces of feedback he got was, "The curse word took away from the presentation." This inspired Jason to write a blog post, "Is it okay to drop an F-bomb in a keynote?" And 80 percent of the commenters said it was fine. Or as Jason puts it, "My whole life is a parental advisory sticker, so I think you know what you're getting if you ask me to speak."

If you stop trying to be something you're not, it lets you focus on being good at your job—which is why you were hired in the first place. But Jason also knows how to walk the line of what's personally expected and what's professionally acceptable. His main job is to tell the story of content marketing on LinkedIn and help people to understand LinkedIn. So although he wears KISS and Slayer shirts to work (and he's found out that people are disappointed if "the rock 'n' roll marketing guy" wears J. Crew), he did tell his boss that if his dress ever presented a problem, he could button up if needed.

It's important to embrace your identity and not conform, but you also want to do that without letting it distract from your work. And though Jason brings his personality to his profession, he also knows what to keep private, such as his views on politics, current events, and other controversial topics. Jason points out, "It's about being smart—you have to know the rules of engagement. Every day, brands make stupid mistakes on social media by sharing something that someone thinks is funny—until it comes back to bite them." Jason doesn't answer questions about the future of the company, because he knows his job is to talk about the benefits and the strengths of content marketing on LinkedIn. He quotes one of his favorite (fictional) bands: "Spinal Tap says, 'There's a fine line between being stupid and clever.' And I think brands straddle that line every single day."

At the end of the day, Jason's biggest advantage is that he truly understands and respects LinkedIn's audience. "It's the world's largest professional network," he says, "so I don't post my recaps from the Slayer concert on LinkedIn. There's a professional mindset we need to think of. People spend time on Facebook, but they invest time in LinkedIn. So I think it's two different mindsets, and that's how I walk the line."

You don't want to stick out like a sore thumb at your company, but you probably don't have to be just another identical cog in the machine. When you have the option, select companies to work with that don't enforce conformity among employees. There are plenty of companies that fit this description, and the number of such employers is growing.

At the same time, we think it feels a little hypocritical to talk about the importance of consistent branding and then encourage individuals to undermine the corporate brands that support them. The key thing here is to think about your company's core traits, and determine how their values fit in with you own. For example, if you work for Travelocity, and then consistently tweet or blog about how you think travel is overrated, there's a clear disconnect.

As an individual, demonstrate how your personal brand plays into your role at the company and how it is beneficial for both parties. If this is not the case, then modify your brand while at work, or decide if the company is even the right place for you. If you find yourself working at a company whose brand you don't believe in, that's a sign that it's not the best fit.

Individualism—the concept that the "rights, beliefs and responsibilities of each person should be more prominent than the rights, beliefs and responsibilities of a group"[3]—provides the basis for entrepreneurship and innovation. In businesses that promote a greater level of individualism, managers give employees greater latitude in terms of how and when they get their work done. Employees typically have the opportunity to not only voice individual opinions, but to have those opinions respected.

Promoting individualism at work can lead to some healthy competition. When each worker stands out more on their own merits, he or she will tend to exhibit higher levels of creativity, innovation, and conflict resolution. Many companies are seeing the benefits of promoting individualism, and encouraging it more.

Letting Your People Shine

Ultimately, Jason Miller encourages his team to be themselves and bring their personalities to the office. The way he sees it, if you don't know who you are and who you want to be, and you don't have an online identity to back that up, that could be the deciding factor in whether you get the next position, promotion, speaking gig, whatever your goal is—or not.

If you're managing others, do you let your employees allow their personal brands to shine? Allowing your people high degrees of latitude in building their own brand helps you hold onto quality people who might otherwise be tempted to leave. Replacement costs for strong talent can be costly both in terms of finances and in the time it takes to recruit and train a replacement.

Another reason to give your people latitude is that having this type of freedom gives people higher degrees of job satisfaction. According to Pew Foundation research, 39 percent of entrepreneurs report they experience "complete" job satisfaction, compared to 28 percent of those who have a boss.[4] Making employees feel as if they don't have a boss restricting their personal branding initiatives can lead to greater job satisfaction, encourage employee loyalty, and boost productivity.

If you (and your team) enjoy high degrees of latitude, make sure you don't take advantage of this freedom. Your work can't take a back seat to your personal projects when you're on company time.

When Corporate and Personal Brand are One and the Same

Entrepreneurs and small business owners will often face an interesting problem: What if you're doing business under your own name? Can a guy named Brandon Jennings have a firm named Brandon Jennings, LLC while keeping distinctive personal and professional brands? To be honest: not really. There's too much name confusion there, and one of those identities is going to overtake the other.

This applies even when you name a company after just one of your names. That's part of the reason why Jeremy never considered a name like Goldman, LLC for Firebrand Group. He wanted to be clear that the company stood apart from his personal brand, especially because he knew he would soon be making significant hires who would each add their own distinctive flavor to the mix. Claudia

Lebenthal, who runs Style of Sport, didn't want the name Lebenthal to be within her digital property. She wanted it to be clear that—although she represents the Style of Sport brand—she and the company are not the same exact thing.

Striking the Right Balance

How do you balance the need to be yourself with the need to embody your brand at all times? You don't have to give yourself a headache in the attempt, but your audience will expect you to support your brand's main tenets. If you're starting an organic food company, you can't ever post a photo of a nonorganic corn muffin or you'll wind up mocked on the front page of *Gawker*. You need to be aware that eyes will be on you, and people's focus on your actions will only be more pronounced as your brand grows.

Those who know you well will be able to accept a more multifaceted or nuanced view of you. This means that on closely held social platforms, such as your personal Facebook page—provided you share with only a smaller network—you can be more off-brand and less focused. People need a little variety to stay interesting; would you unfollow someone if they posted the same thing every day? Yeah, so would we.

Juggling Person Brand Identity
With Gordon Ramsay

Michelin-rated chef, restaurateur, and TV personality Gordon Ramsay is a nice, level-headed person. Yes, really. He just knows how to present himself in a manner that his audience will enjoy.

Chef Ramsay is one of the clearest examples of keeping separate brand identities. He is quite open about how his on-screen persona—the red-faced, livid man screaming about food that is "F*CKING RAWWWWW!"—is just an act. Just look at his work on *MasterChef Junior*. Instead of ranting and sprinkling expletives as liberally as sea salt, Ramsay showed his more sensitive, mentoring side when working with kid chefs.

Ramsay plays the role of a domineering and chronically frustrated chef in American shows because it draws viewers. The audience of *Hell's Kitchen* expects drama, jump cuts, action, heroes, and villains. In Britain, audiences want to see a talented man make food, so more moderate and skill-focused shows like *The F Word* and Gordon's home cooking show are successful.

Ramsay has a crucial element that's often the solution to any brand issue: the skills to back up his actions. He's a celebrity chef with a very impressive résumé, and he's worked in and owned top restaurants. Ramsay is passionate and a hard worker, and he's paid his dues. It shows in the way he approaches food in shows where he plays the straight man. He is eager to learn from others, humble, and appreciative of other people's talent.

Gordon also has an ace in the hole: Whatever else you can say about him, he has used his fame for good. He's worked to expose corrupt practices in the food industry, especially where shark fin harvesting is concerned. Given Ramsay's humanitarian work, it feels rather thin when people try to bring him down for his cartoonish behavior on certain cooking dramas.

Philanthropic work should not be something you only do simply to make yourself more attractive and marketable, but it is undeniable that it helps put things in perspective. Most negative feedback you receive in regards to your profession will be overshadowed if you prove yourself to be a good, generous person.

Past Iterations of Your Personal Brand

Before Jeremy went off to business school, he had a going-away party that included many friends, including his girlfriend at the time, Victoria (now his wife). Some of his high school friends, who had drifted away in the seven years since graduation, decided to come to the party. Not necessarily to wish Jeremy well; they wanted to confirm that Victoria did, in fact, exist. That's because in 8th grade, when

Jeremy was highly unpopular, he made up a girlfriend. Whether or not Jeremy deserved to have that reputation intact 12 years later isn't really the point; what matters is that former acquaintances still had that association.

You may work with people who knew you when you were a different person—either from earlier in your career, or even as far back as college or high school. There are perceptions of you that others hold onto from a long time ago, when you were a very different person. When you find yourself working with someone who holds the past against you, it's important to identify it. Then, decide if you can work in that situation. First impressions do matter, and there are some people whose opinion of you will be frozen for all time.

One of Jeremy's mentors knew him back when he worked for her as a technology-first marketer. When he transitioned through his career to more of a branding and communications-first, technology-second approach, she still saw him as what he had been a decade prior—and because of that she felt less inclined to collaborate with him on branding projects. Knowing that this was someone particularly strong-willed, Jeremy felt it wise to keep the relationship, but not waste the time trying to change her opinion.

Identify Inconsistencies

Beyond reconciling your past self with your present identity, there may also be inconsistencies within your current identity—and that isn't always a problem. It's possible to resolve these incongruities and even work them to your advantage. For one, you can do this by leaning into them. If you embrace contradiction, that's interesting, and can help you stand out better from the crowd. As Alyssa Gelbard, career advice expert, says:

> Little quirks are great. There are probably a million different people with your job, but when you show this whole other part of yourself, you give a new dimension to your identity. There can be benefits in the different aspects of your personality—like adaptability or discipline—which

can be applied to work situations. At the end of the day, what's going to make you stand out? Don't lead with your unusual traits, but if you have something memorable, I would consider putting it in your additional information. Just make sure you have relevant professional skills as well.[5]

If you're going to embrace the contradictions and idiosyncrasies that make you who you are—you know, a unique snowflake—make sure you can do so without losing control of your messaging. You don't want to be known as the guy who shoots rock 'n' roll concerts with a side of B2B marketing; you want to be known as the guy who is a serious B2B marketer with a side of rock 'n' roll photography. Balance is key, and you don't want your side projects to overshadow your main focus.

We talked to Gabrielle Archambault, a former coworker of Jeremy's, when she was trying to figure out how to balance some of the diverse areas on her resume. Gabrielle has had an interesting career: Trained in formal art at the renowned Pratt Institute, she used her background there to get a career managing the creation of fake tattoos for top-tier Hollywood productions. There were even rumors that Gabrielle worked on the body art for David Fincher's version of *The Girl with the Dragon Tattoo*. At some point, however, she made a case for taking over her company's social media efforts, and excelled in her new role. Pretty soon, she was a rising digital marketing executive, overseeing millions in e-commerce revenue.

When updating her résumé, Gabrielle felt she had a dilemma: Should she mention her art-centric experience, or leave it off? On the one hand, she felt that it was a key part of what defined her. On the other hand, did the art and tattoo production experience draw attention to her unconventional rise through the ranks? Although she was considered to be quite talented, she did technically have less experience in digital marketing compared to some at her level.

Gabrielle felt that her inconsistent background might make her seem less authentic as a digital marketer. The truth, however, is that her interesting background reinforced her authenticity as a multifaceted and adaptable talent, and helped her to stand out from other professionals.

If you're in a similar situation, keep in mind that interesting experiences in your past and unexpected character quirks can work to your benefit, provided they don't detract from the attributes and experience you're trying to highlight.

Some Challenges Specific to Women

While we're on the topic of becoming more comfortable with a new venture, let's talk about how this can be especially challenging for more than half the world's population. We've had the fortune to work alongside a lot of talented women in the course of our careers (not to mention that one of us would like to think she's a talented woman), and we've noticed that women can feel more hesitant to put themselves out there than men. There's also the clichéd-but-true pressure that many women feel to "have it all": to not just juggle multiple personal identities, but to balance their home/family life with career goals and professional responsibilities.

One friend put it like this: "For most guys to feel qualified to do something, they only need to be about 60 percent certain. Most women feel like they have to be 150 percent capable before they'll take the leap." Even before Sheryl Sandberg's *Lean In* was published, the difference between how men and women act and interact in a business setting was a hot topic. In our culture, men tend to feel more comfortable being the big personality in the room, whereas women might have been encouraged to play a supporting versus a leading role. This is a generalization, of course—we know plenty of assertive women, and more than a few guys who keep a low profile in the conference room. But it's true that our society still tends to tell girls and women that they need to be polite and people-pleasers, not confrontational, aggressive, or self-promoting.

At the beginning of your career, this might be true. Nobody wants an intern who thinks she knows how to run the place. But the game changes when you're making the transition into a leadership role or running your own brand. Your identity matters, and it matters that you have a recognizable one. In this context, being present and visible—both in person and on social platforms—isn't attention-seeking. It's a job requirement. Think of having an active brand as adding a major skill to your résumé.

Sarah Kugelman, founder of Skyn Iceland, shares: "I think being a female entrepreneur is unique. I have been a member of a group of female entrepreneurs for 10 years now, and we meet every month to talk a lot about our businesses, how we approach things differently, and how we manage employees. Between hiring and mentoring other women and the way that I look at the business, being a woman impacts my point of view and what I do."[6]

We feel that being a woman impacts *more* than your point of view. If you're a woman, that's often part of your *brand*, whether you intend for it to be or not. Depending on your situation, it can be a hindrance or a bonus. Unfortunately, many women still face issues with disrespect and preconceptions about their ability to do their job. If a woman takes on a traditionally masculine role (this includes being a business leader), or is in a business where she is a minority, then she often has to deal with the fact that others will expect more of her than they would of men.

This can be an advantage, however. If you prove yourself capable and professional, you are admired for both the qualities themselves and for overcoming these expectations. Women often have to worry about something else that men typically do not: changing their name. Considering we are advocating discipline and consistency when it comes to branding yourself, there's a bit of an unfair disadvantage that women encounter as a result of changing their brand identity when they're already engaged in their careers.

Up until a few years ago, Ali was known as Ali Butterfass personally and professionally. Driver's license, passport, college, employment history—you name it. Then, she got married. Now, whether we're socializing or taking care of business, you can call her Ali B. Zagat.

There's no rule that said she had to change her name. The married-vs.-maiden-name debate is one that has no winner, as far as we're both concerned. It's your name. It's your decision.

But let's say that, like Ali, you've established a reputation around your birth name. She tried keeping personal and professional separate for a while, using her given name at work and her married name everywhere else.

Unfortunately, this split identity can be confusing. Ali had a credit card under her married name, but the "other Ali" was getting the paycheck. She introduced herself as Ali Z. to people in a social setting; trying to switch between the two makes it sound like she didn't know who she was. And in effect, she didn't.

While a rose by any other name would smell as sweet, in our socially saturated culture, everyone has a message to share and a voice to share it with. That makes it important to establish who you are. Every picture, video, and line of text broadcasts your personality and your priorities, and best practices include maintaining a cohesive whole. Once Ali had made the decision to transition to her married name, she knew that she had some cleanup work to do. It seemed overwhelming, but all her social media accounts got an overhaul:

Twitter: Ali came online in the pseudonym age of the Internet, so her Twitter handle was @mmeflutterby instead of her name. And though you can change your username, Ali actually kind of liked this relic from her past. Ultimately, she switched over to @alibzagat for consistency's sake. In addition, she edited her profile to display her new name. The name in your profile can be different from your username (old, new, real, or imagined), so this is one fix you don't even need 140 characters to describe.

Facebook: Another simple change, accessed from the settings menu. Set both your name and your username (Ali kept her maiden name in the name field to make it easier for old connections to find her). She actually had more trouble getting her non-social-media-savvy spouse to confirm that they were updating their relationship from engaged to married.

(Note: Be aware that once you change your name, Facebook will not let you change it again for the next 60 days. So make sure that your chosen moniker is exactly the way you want it, because you'll be stuck with it for two months.)

Instagram: Ali really appreciated that you can edit your name and your handle here, too. It was even simpler than snapping a selfie.

E-mail: This was Ali's one exception, as she didn't want to ask everyone she had ever met to switch over to a new address, or stop using the old address and miss an important message. However, Ali did set up a new account to start using, and set one account to forward to the other. She also updated her display name.

Website: Depending on how comfortable you are with Web hosting and what platform you use, this can seem a bit complicated. If you have a WordPress, Tumblr, or other site with a custom URL, for example, you'll need to check if [Yournewname].com is available. Thankfully, both Ali's maiden and married names are relatively uncommon, so she was able to secure her new site. Ali checked for a couple of different permutations of her name, too. Similar to her e-mail, once she had the new site ready to launch, she set the old site to automatically forward visitors to the updated account.

Résumé: In addition to the copy you keep on your computer, if you've uploaded a sample résumé anywhere be sure to change your name for consistency.

LinkedIn: Like Facebook, you can set what you want to use, both as an identity and for the link to your profile page. Same rose, different name.

Portfolio: Ali uses Contently, which also lets you set your name and custom URL.

Compared to updating your passport, Social Security card, and driver's license, most social platforms make it easy for you to provide information for the new you. And speaking of those governmental institutions, have you thought about who you are for your 401(k), health insurance, stock options, utility accounts, and other financial paper trails? Just as every marriage is different, every company has a unique approach to changing sensitive data. Some companies require you to send in a proof of identity, like a copy of your marriage license. Others require you to go through your employer's HR department.

Ali imagined changing her name would be a big deal, and a big time commitment, so she was pleasantly surprised when it was not as labor-intensive as she had feared. Yes, it can have an impact on your personal branding, but we leave that up to you to weigh the pros against the cons.

Chapter 11

Avoiding and Recovering
From a Branding Disaster

Most Common Hazards of Digital Engagement

We see it across LinkedIn, Facebook, and Twitter every day: despite trying to grow a strong digital presence and personal brand, many people inadvertently paint unflattering pictures of themselves. They post a status complaining about their commute to work, or brag about their new car, or list their detailed schedule for the day in an effort to look important. If you're like us, you roll your eyes because, who cares, really?

When you're building your personal brand across all your social media channels, it's important to best represent yourself in a positive light, and not detract from your public image due to "unforced errors." Some of these mistakes are obvious, and yet even trained professionals make them from time to time.

What's the good news? Most of them are easily avoidable. Here are the four we work hardest to sidestep:

1. **Being inauthentic.**

   There was a point in which the millions of people who follow George Takei on Facebook thought he was a one-man joke machine. But when Takei's ghostwriter came clean, the former Star Trek legend's reputation took a major hit.

   Chances are you're not a beloved actor, but being perceived as inauthentic could set you back big time. Being fake is one of the biggest turn-offs when you meet someone in person, and the same applies to our digital interactions. People can tell when you're being genuine, and the number one form of branding self-sabotage is trying to be someone you're not.

   This sort of inauthenticity occurs when things are happening too quickly for us to keep up. We achieve a certain reputation that increases our popularity, and we just roll with it, appealing to that audience without actually working toward the identity they assume we inhabit. But when it becomes clear that we do not reflect the reality we're projecting, people can turn quickly, and that's when things get ugly.

2. **Lacking originality when sharing links and updates.**

   Whether you're tweeting, sharing posts on Facebook, or connecting with someone on LinkedIn, it's important to customize your message and not always resort to using that platform's default text.

   People notice when you take the time to write a personal note or message, and doing so will immediately set you apart. It says a few things: you're polite, you pay attention to detail, and you go the extra mile—all of which adds to the success of your personal brand.

   You can't just pump out retweets, shares, and offers to connect; you have to have something of substance on the back end. Do your research and contribute quality content. Don't just parrot others who have already shown promise in those areas.

3. **Forgetting to take your digital brand offline.**

   This is one of the most common mistakes. If you don't leverage the brand you're building via digital channels into growing your offline reputation, you're missing a big opportunity.

   Think about it: most people fall in love with a celebrity after seeing them in an interview because it showcases their personality off-screen. Whether you're engaged in a Twitter chat, a lively LinkedIn Groups discussion, or a debate in your favorite blog's comments section, if you have the opportunity to meet your connections in person, we say jump on it!

   People who want to update their brand are often so caught up in the rush to do so that they neglect this aspect. They want to get the process over with as quickly as possible, and more ground-level, IRL interactions seem like small peanuts compared to the power of online branding moves. But depth complements breadth, and a few quality interactions can turn into genuine word-of-mouth promotion from those you interact with during these meet-ups.

   What's the worst that will happen? If you don't love one another, you've wasted an hour of your time over coffee. If you do hit it off, you just might develop a professional connection that lasts for years. Face-to-face interactions will only serve to strengthen the relationships you've begun online.

4. **Thinking it's all about you.**

   Contrary to popular belief, your personal brand is not all about you. Although the name itself may suggest this, personal branding is a distillation of all your defining traits and characteristics. In that sense, personal branding is—in part—about how you can help others.

The last thing you want to be known as is self-centered or self-promotional. Being generous to people in your network is one of the best ways to build relationships and your reputation. This is a common issue with personal branding in general, but it gets worse as you up the volume in conjunction with your brand update and push your new persona. If you're not careful, you may also end up unintentionally pushing the idea that you are self-obsessed.

Damage Control

Even the savviest professional may slip and have an "open mouth, insert foot" moment. If you've made a blunder, what should you do next?

Proactively addressing the problem is a key part of the solution. All too often, we encounter large corporate brands, as well as personal brands, that refused to admit that they have made a mistake. Generally speaking, the more that somebody digs in and refuses to admit that they've made a mistake, the larger the public outcry will be, and the greater the demands for an apology. Admitting when you are wrong or when you have misspoken, whether it's digitally or in person, tends to quell the vast majority of your critics. There are times when you may want to dig in your heels, but choose your battles wisely.

Enlisting a core group of allies is another key part of the solution. Think of the people who are usually your evangelists, and reach out to them, directly seeking their support. Typically, people who know you well will offer their support via a public statement. When you have some people defending you, the "pile on" mentality that is all too common these days will be less likely to form.

When and How to Apologize

The key to good damage control is, above all, transparency. "Being truthful, even if it makes one look bad, is the quickest way to reduce the length of time spent by media covering an issue or the length of public outrage exhibited on social media," says Robert Zimmerman, the longtime crisis communications executive. "By not telling the truth, the media and public will continue to seek it out, thus prolonging the public attention and exposure of a crisis. Ultimately, if a company or person is found to be 'lying' the truth will come out."[1]

The best thing to do, Robert advocates, is to admit the mistake. If you've made an honest mistake, the public is generally willing to accept and forgive that. It's important not to deflect by giving a crazy reason as to why your mistake occurred. People don't like being treated as if they're stupid. For example, when Brian Williams was caught in a lie about his helicopter being shot at in Iraq, his stated excuse that his memory was foggy damaged his credibility. After all, most people can't imagine forgetting something like that.

If you've brought in outside assistance to help you manage your crisis—or legal counsel if you're *really* in hot water—don't lie or hold back. To effectively create a proper course of action, your team has to know all the facts. Holding back on details is a bad idea approximately 100 percent of the time.

Robert sees one key trait in common with people who successfully lift themselves out of a hole they've dug themselves in, versus those who don't: responsiveness. "The quicker you are to respond and try to be transparent as possible, the better," he says. "Whether people are going to believe you is another thing. The quicker you can get your message out there to the media or bloggers or the world of social media, the better you are."

Besides being transparent, it's imperative to establish a proactive plan to help right the wrong that was committed—or demonstrate how you have learned from your mistake. Your audience wants to see proof of your remorse, otherwise they'll write it off as pure spin.

When admitting a mistake, Robert recommends providing the real reason why you did *what* you did. Your thought process is just as important—if not more important—than the admission. Another thing people get wrong is when they are not willing to accept the reality and gravity of their situation. Or "they try to justify their mistake," he says. "They accept the reality, but aren't willing to face the consequences that they will ultimately have to face, so they try to justify their actions."

Depending on how bad the gaffe is, that will have a major impact on any potential comeback strategy. Usually, it's best to let things die down a bit before you reenter the public spotlight. Whatever you do, don't use your fall from grace as a news hook to regain your career. If you screw up and try to turn it into a positive, there's a good chance you might dig yourself into an even bigger hole.

How to Gracefully Own and Recover From Your Mistakes: Examining Infamous Pitfalls

Every now and then, someone makes a major misstep. These include:

- CeeLo Green, whose reality show was cancelled immediately after he made offensive comments about rape.
- Fashion mogul Kenneth Cole, who has made a multitude of unfortunate comments through the years.

CeeLo came under fire after tweeting about his definition of rape. This was right after he had pleaded no contest to a charge that he had secretly slipped ecstasy to a woman two years prior while they were out to dinner. The woman stated that CeeLo had spiked her drink. The next thing she knew, she woke up naked in a hotel room with him there. What's interesting is that very few fans of CeeLo's were aware of the plea deal. But the entertainer himself actually raised awareness of what had happened, tweeting:

When someone brakes on [sic] a home there is broken glass where is your plausible proof anyone was raped.

Women who have really been raped REMEMBER!!! If someone is passed out they're not even WITH you consciously! So WITH implies consent.

He quickly removed the controversial tweets, going so far as to temporarily delete his account. He later reactivated his account to issue an apology. "I truly and deeply apologize for the comments attributed to me on Twitter," *The Voice* judge and award-winning singer wrote. "Those comments were idiotic, untrue, and not what I believe." Unfortunately for CeeLo, it was too little, too late: he was dropped from multiple concert dates after his controversial remarks on such a serious issue, and his personal brand suffered a long-term, possibly terminal setback.

Another celebrity who isn't a stranger to controversy is Kenneth Cole. In September 2013, when the U.S. was debating entering the Syrian civil war, the fashion designer tweeted the following:

'Boots on the ground' or not, let's not forget about sandals, pumps, and loafers. #Footwear

It's not the first time the designer embroiled himself in controversy, either. Cole has made a name for himself on multiple occasions with his provocative, almost incendiary tweets. In 2011, as the Arab Spring began and protests rose in fervor in Egypt, he tweeted:

Millions are in uproar in #Cairo. Rumor is they heard our new spring collection is now available online... -KC

Later, he deleted this tweet. He apologized, describing it as "insensitive." One might say that being controversial and provocative is an intentional part of his brand—and they'd be right. Still, what's unclear is whether or not this calculated desire to stir controversy adds more to his brand, or if it primarily detracts.

Gloria Huang: Dealing With Adversity

Gloria Huang has dealt with branding crises for a large part of her career. So you'd think she'd be the last person to cause one, right? We'll take a look at how she put her PR skills to work when she ended up on the defensive.

Gloria started out in crisis consulting firm TMG Strategies (now McGinn and Company), where she quickly learned that crisis management entailed "planning 99 percent of the time and then executing 1 percent of the time."[2] This involves developing a communications plan, training her team thoroughly and then, when the time comes, getting the team to follow her plan to the letter.

As Gloria points out, social media is still such a complex and unpredictable field, even to those with experience. "No one was an expert in social media when I started my career, and no one still is, really," says Gloria. "When you are working in an area in which things are rapidly changing and evolving, you don't have that many true experts."

But if no one is an expert, how do you find success, or deal with setbacks? For Gloria, the answer is rooted in having a highly academic mindset and constantly learning. That sort of adaptability and open approach allows her to be flexible when she encounters a situation she could never have planned for. At the same time, Gloria enjoys looking for opportunities to apply what she has learned to the real world. The drive to keep learning, tailoring, and adapting to the changing landscape is crucial.

Gloria learned a painful lesson about setbacks in what was perhaps the most damaging move of her professional career—an incident in which an easily understandable mistake led to some big consequences. In 2011, Gloria was working as a social media specialist for the Red Cross, which included managing their Twitter account. She had done a great job with the position, until one night in February. At 11:24 p.m. on the 15th, Gloria intended to send out a Tweet from her personal Twitter account, saying:

Ryan found 2 more 4 bottle packs of Dogfish Head's Midas Touch beer... When we drink we do it right #gettingslizzerd.

But what happened was—you guessed it—Gloria did not send out the tweet to her own friends, but instead mistakenly broadcast the message to the Red Cross's 268,000 followers.

The effect was immediate. The tweet blew up, with many joke tweets echoing Huang's #gettingslizzered. It could have been a setback for the organization and led to some really negative press.

Gloria and the rest of the team leapt into action, admirably trying to find a way to make the best out of the situation. Soon after the original tweet went out, the Red Cross followed up the misstep with this:

We've deleted the rogue tweet but rest assured the Red Cross is sober and we've confiscated the keys.

Gloria defused the situation by casting it in a humorous light, and actually ended up raising extra donations as #gettingslizzered became a trending topic and positive awareness of Red Cross's deftness at recovering from pitfalls increased. Instead of outrage, the incident created good will, and was ultimately a beneficial event for the organization.

Gloria knew from experience how that first, initial reaction you have to something strongly affects the outcome. "Is your reaction to clamp down on it, to try to sweep it under the rug? Or is it to try to embrace it?" When social media turns ugly, myriad examples have demonstrated the powerful remedial effects of assuming responsibility and working through an issue head-on.

What could have been an embarrassing moment for Gloria was quickly turned around. With a forward-looking approach, she was able to work past her mistake and treat it as a learning experience rather than a detriment to—or the end of—her career.

With the rise of digital media, every single thing you do is under a microscope. The slightest error has the potential to blow up in your face. But when something does misfire, you can learn from these experiences and pick up valuable insights. That's almost impossible to teach; when you have actually been in it and lived it, you learn things that somebody else might not be able to.

People have gotten so used to feeling like they have insight into every detail of other's lives and what is going on with organizations and companies because they can follow everyone on social media. Because of that mindset, both companies and individuals are much more guarded with how they phrase their communications and what they choose to share. The assumption is that, just by following someone on Facebook or Twitter, you really know every intimate detail about their lives. But you're only following what's posted on digital and social platforms. You'll never know exactly what's going on beneath the surface.

Gloria laughs when reflecting on the questions people asked after her accidental tweet:

> I think it was funny that some of these people would always come to me and say, "Tell me the real story. What happened when you messed up?" And I would always tell them this positive story about how my team was 100 percent behind me and I felt like I had a lot of support. I felt like I learned a whole lot and we were able to turn it into a positive, because there was just an assumption that we would work together.

Not everyone has a story like Gloria's, and not every issue has a similar background. One of the major contributing factors in recovering from a problem like that—especially in the long term—is continuing to talk about why this happened, how everyone worked together, and what that really taught you. Don't look back with shame and regret; look forward with experience and optimism.

Failure in General

You could make the argument that Gloria failed. And we'd make the argument that not only is that okay, but that the experience made her a better professional going forward. Part of what's made Gaby Dalkin—of *What's Gaby Cooking*, from earlier chapters—successful is her ability to recover from setbacks. When she came out with her cookbook, she had high ambitions, including booking every morning show. In particular, she wanted to be on *The Ellen DeGeneres Show*. "My publicist was saying, 'You know these are kind of outrageous requests, right?' I was saying 'We've just got to go for it.'"[3]

Gaby ended up not being on *Ellen*, which was a disappointment. But it was something she bounced back from, reasoning that it will happen when it's fated to happen. "And," she adds, "drowning my sorrows in a grilled cheese sandwich really helps. I mean, that really helps."

Chapter 12

Retargeting and Updating Your Brand

There was a year or two when Bradford Shellhammer was in the process of building Fab into one of the hottest startups in the U.S., and he had a feeling of invincibility. Sounds great, no? But in hindsight, that feeling was damaging because he felt he knew better than a lot of other people. Having to swallow a "humble pill" has made him a much nicer and collaborative person.

"I know what it's like to feel like you have something in this world, and then it's gone. It's a really humbling experience," he says.[1] The only way he can explain how he felt when Fab started experiencing severe difficulties, and his relationship with the company crumbling, is this: The closest he felt to that is when his father died. His humbling experience taught him some important lessons: "All of the accomplishments in the world, in the end, mean nothing. The only thing that will matter is how you made them feel."

Just like Bradford used his experience at Fab to better himself, it's a good idea to take a look at your brand from time to time and do a check-up. Is everything working well, or is your brand in dire need of repairs? Sometimes the state of things will be obvious, and sometimes they may not be so cut and dry. In this chapter we will outline the warning signs that it's time to fix up your brand, so you'll know what to look for and decide if it's time to make some tweaks or even significant changes. There are many challenges you may face when you attempt to fix your brand, and a lot of different factors you will have to consider in order to ensure the transition goes as smoothly as possible. A full audit of your brand across various social platforms is just one of a number of solutions which we'll cover here.

Whether they like it or not, most people will need to reinvent and reimagine themselves at some point in their careers. It could be because they decide to change jobs or maybe—unfortunately and all too common—they get laid off and need to come up with a new plan. Most people will face this situation eventually, whether by choice or by chance. However, on one level or another, we're all essentially reinventing ourselves in small ways as we go. As you advance in your career, you're naturally making progress along the way. You improve your existing skills, learn new ones, and fine-tune your resume. It's easier than ever to become obsolete, and a constant evolution is necessary if you want to stay relevant. It takes, at most, six months to get out of date. We need to embrace a mentality of continuous learning and be ready for regular periods of reinvention. What brings in revenue, or drives your business today, may be very different than what will make a big difference to your bottom line in a year. When you're self-employed or relying on your personal brand in some way for your livelihood, success is largely predicated on self-promotion, in the style demanded by the time.

Revising Your Brand and Yourself

Maybe you tried to market yourself as one thing and it didn't work out. Or you might be a retiree reentering the workforce, or trying to add new skills to stay relevant. Now, who or what are you?

How do you want to reinvent yourself? You need to have a clear idea of your end goal so you can plan accordingly. What are your interests? Sometimes, a career pivot can be as easy as thinking about where your interests lie and following them accordingly.

Ask yourself: "What are my particular specialties and areas of expertise?" Slowing down and taking the time to ask yourself something like that will help you acknowledge something that you've always been innately good at, but haven't thought of as a career possibility, or monetized in any other way. Jeremy's wife, Victoria, for example, is an expert organizer. If she ever left her field of art provenance, she knows she has the potential to pivot into personal organization consulting.

Taking a Class

Taking a class can be a great way to pivot. We think of this as continuing education for your personal brand, a chance to refresh yourself and reposition your talents. You've got a ton of options in this arena: You can find a traditional class or an online-only class, or even go for a new degree. Taking an online class is easier than one might think. One good place to start is Coursera, an education platform that teams up with top universities and organizations all over the world. Its stated mission is to offer courses online for anyone to take, for free.

Trying Something Entirely New

What do you do if you're a standout in one area but want to rebrand to get known in another? If you've ever seen *Parks and Recreation*, the genius sitcom starring Amy Poehler, you might be familiar with Ron Swanson's alter ego, Duke Silver. Ron, played beautifully by Nick Offerman, invents the Duke Silver persona so that he can play jazz saxophone at Cozy's Bar in Eagleton, Indiana. Why does Ron go through all the trouble of concealing his identity? He's so well known as a curmudgeon in Pawnee that the suave Duke Silver persona just doesn't fit with his character.

It may sound counterintuitive, but in some cases your past successes can work against you—kind of like what Ron encounters. This principle applies for nonfictional entities as well. Take J.K. Rowling, for instance, who publishes non–Harry Potter works under a pseudonym.

Volunteering and Boards

Sometimes you might realize that what you were trying to do with your life is just not right for you anymore. If that's the situation you find yourself in, you might become distraught, wondering how you can possibly pivot this late in the game into doing something that really speaks to you. Who will give you a chance to do what you now realize is your dream?

Well, one thing that you can do to build experience in your new target area is volunteering your time and skills in a professional capacity. You may often think about volunteering outside of your company, but you can also find ways to volunteer within your company on projects that you wouldn't otherwise be exposed to. This helps you pick up new skill sets, and also lets you flesh out your résumé in the direction that you are trying to go. It can be instrumental in helping you find a job in the field that you are looking to get into. Some companies have boards to plan extracurricular activities, such as company outings or sports leagues. If you've been pigeonholed at work and are only known for one particular thing, volunteering on a board may help you get known for your other attributes.

That's the situation that Jeremy found himself in when he was launching a luxury division for Unilever. He had primarily been the digital marketing expert at all of the firms where he had worked, but he wanted an opportunity to do more. More specifically, he wanted a chance to help others build digital marketing careers for themselves. When the brand he was working on, iluminage, hit product development delays—which pushed back the launch of the brand and also freed up Jeremy's schedule—he decided to do something about it and volunteer, in a sense. He started a digital networking group called Mosaic to connect digital marketing professionals of all levels so that they could support and get advice from one another. The main qualifier for joining was that you had to be somebody interested in giving back to others. At present moment, Mosaic has more than 300 members and is going strong.

Another thing that Jeremy started doing around this time was to offer personal branding consultations to mentees who were earlier on in their careers, or those in the middle of their career who were looking to rebrand themselves in order to find new roles or industries. Jeremy didn't charge for this service, figuring that at the start especially, just having the experience of being a personal branding coach was reward enough. Helping so many in their careers is part of what prompted him to join up with Ali to write this book. It might not have been the most profitable enterprise, but it allowed Jeremy to develop his skills in the process and provide him with a lot of positive "client" experiences—not to mention the satisfaction of having helped others get their start in the field.

Volunteering allows you the opportunity to put something new on your résumé that shows how dedicated you are to moving in a particular professional direction. Another great way to show your dedication is to join a nonprofit board. If you're passionate about something, a nonprofit board allows you to have a major impact.

Job Shadowing

Of course, many of us aren't positive whether a particular direction is the right one. In a situation like this, job shadowing might be a good option. This entails following another professional around and seeing what a day in their shoes might be like. (Some of the people that you have informational interviews with might be able to accommodate such a request.) If you're going to shadow somebody at their job, it's a great opportunity to ask questions about what you've just experienced to see whether or not it is the norm in that particular company and occupation. Job shadowing doesn't have to be limited to an occupation that you don't know anything about; you can also focus on a senior executive at your existing company. There's a good chance they're not getting that many requests from people who want to shadow them for a day, so your request will likely be flattering and you'll have at least a small shot at success.

Whether you're looking to job shadow someone senior or merely network with them, there are two traits that go very well together: pluckiness and respect. Pluck, or determination, is a very desirable trait. We have plenty of stories about people who tried to network with us, but didn't put any effort into getting a meeting onto our schedules—or who gave up far too easily. Jobs are difficult, and if somebody abandons the networking stage, it's hard to imagine that he or she will be an amazing employee. Therefore, pluck is a terrific personal branding attribute. Respect is another trait that will serve you well, and it's a great complement to pluckiness. After all, no busy senior executive wants to take time out of their busy schedule to network with somebody who thinks that they already know everything—or who acts entitled rather than appreciative. Strike the right balance between determination and understanding of somebody else's calendar.

When you are brainstorming companies or people that you want to work for, head to LinkedIn and do some research. Chances are you'll be able to find somebody you know who can put you in touch with the relevant contact.

Maximizing Your Efforts

When you put together your résumé, don't waste space on the things that anybody could do. Instead, focus on your talents and areas where you think you can provide the most value and flesh those out. Whenever possible, put numbers next to achievements at your previous occupations. For example, "lowered marketing costs" is not nearly as impressive as "lowered marketing costs by over 35 percent," because it actually measures how *well* you did *what* you did.

Taking a Sabbatical

Reputations can be fickle, and it's very possible that you'll end up with no idea what you did to ruin your image. If you earn yourself a bad reputation, it's nearly impossible to erase that blemish, even if you move into a different field.

One good idea, though, is to take a little bit of a break between your existing career and what you were hoping to do next. This doesn't have to be such a big break—after all, long absences on a résumé are difficult to explain away—but even a short trip to clear your head will help give you a new perspective. This also gives any lingering negative reputations or incidents a chance to die down.

Doing Your Research When Pivoting

Sometimes we don't realize how lucky we are to be living in an age where just about anything can be researched using your favorite search engine. Using LinkedIn and other platforms to review the backgrounds of successful individuals that you would like to emulate is relatively easy to learn, and not really that difficult to master. Let's say you're interested in one day serving in the U.S. House of Representatives: You can do a survey of 10 Representatives who serve the part of the country where you are situated and review their path to power. That doesn't mean it's the only way to join their ranks, but it does shed light on one or two key paths that might make the most sense for you to explore.

In case you don't know exactly whose career to review, some of your favorite periodicals can help. Some of our go-tos are *Inc.* magazine, *Fast Company* magazine, *Fortune* magazine, and *The New York Times.* Try to figure out which publications are best for you. Long flights are one of the best times to go on reading binges. Instead of taking uncomfortable naps, try to examine every page—not just the interviews with the leading figures. We've even received great ideas from, believe it or not, the ads.

Of course, this type of research doesn't necessarily reinforce that you were right to admire the careers that you were researching. Let's say you were interested in becoming a lumberjack and you noticed that the life expectancy of the typical lumberjack was 52 years old. That might convince you to go to another field. However, if you're not persuaded otherwise, you will get more of a feeling for how that field operates. Maybe you were exploring careers in which people tend to be very decisive, but you've previously gotten feedback that you are anything but. Although this could convince you that it's not the right field for you, it might just let you know that you have to start developing those skills.

Also, for better or for worse, jargon is sometimes a barrier to getting into certain fields. This type of language dominates certain professions, and can be one way of letting people in the industry know who belongs and who doesn't. Doing your research can help you determine which words to use to establish credibility and show that you belong, even though—for now—you haven't yet completely earned it. This way, you can go up to a research scientist, or someone else in a specialized field, and show that you've done your homework instead of asking very basic questions about the profession.

Rebranding

Beauty may be skin deep, but a good brand goes far below the surface. It has a story, a purpose, and an underlying philosophy. You need to set the groundwork and make a strong foundation before you build your skyscraper. When deciding how you're going to rebrand yourself, you have to think about what kind of image you're trying to create for your audience and how the audience is going to interpret your reinvention.

When you rebrand, you're not just designing a new brand; you're leaving an old one. You have to consider what you're giving up when you do so, in terms of clients, contacts, or other elements specific to your particular brand or market. Of course, if you're rebranding yourself in order to recover from a negative image, the pros probably outweigh the cons, but you have to consider the tradeoff.

That said, you don't want to leave everything behind. You have to look at how to bring along the positive aspects of your own brand, and incorporate them into your new identity. If you're coming from a background doing intense competitive analysis, and your interest in PR has made you decide to switch careers, position yourself as a PR professional who also has impressive skills to research competitive firms.

Chances are you're not the only element that's changing; when you rebrand yourself, your audience shifts as well. Not everyone who liked your old brand will like the new one, whereas others, who might not have been interested in your brand before, may find something in your new identity that speaks to them. Unless you are shifting specifically for a ripe audience, chances are you are going to take a bit of a hit at first. But with time, the new audience will probably surpass what you had before the brand change.

When you rebrand, you have to reshape your ideas as well. If you approach things exactly how you did with your old brand, you may find that your strategy isn't working. What works for one market, one audience, or one brand may not work for another, even if you're in a similar field or position. A good personal brand is rigid in its presentation, but flexible in its application. Though stability is key when you're established, you might want to be a little more malleable when you're just getting settled. Audience feedback is particularly crucial at this stage; listening to them can help you develop your brand effectively so that it is well-molded to the community by the time it solidifies.

Start early; no, start earlier than that. If you suddenly drop your old brand, neither you nor your audience will be able to adapt quickly and effectively. Rebranding happens while your old brand is still active and before your new brand is announced; it takes a lot of work behind the scenes to transition your brand, and you don't want the audience to see you scrambling. There doesn't have to be a big reveal.

Does Starting Over Really Mean Starting Over?

One fear that many professionals have when rebranding themselves is that they have spent years cultivating a reputation in their field, and now they have to start from square one. This simply isn't the case. If you have developed a reputation for being good at one thing, your contacts will be more inclined to believe you are good at whatever career you have chosen to move toward. Although the world is not divided up between people who are great at everything and people who are bad at everything, it's a natural psychological phenomenon that makes humans more inclined to see others in this manner. Your status and credibility are more portable from one discipline to another than you might think.

Now that we know about this phenomenon, let's take advantage of it by building upon previous experiences and the confidence we have amassed from those successes.

Narrow things down to specifics and consider your target audience. Will your potential audience be companies? Will it be individuals? Are you looking to work primarily with other social media professionals or people who don't have a lot of social media experience? Something else? Keep in mind that different audiences will be interested in different topics, so try to tailor your ideas and the way you think of this to the audience that you want to reach out to. Also, keep in mind what your specialty is, what your niche is going to be, what are you going to own, what you can do better than most other people, and what you do that nobody else does. Think, too, about timing. When will you interact with your audience? What is the best time for you to tweet? What is the best time for you to send e-mails? What is the best time for you to make a blog post? For this, you're probably going to have to play with some testing and see when you get the most traffic and when you get the most responses.

You also want to think about where. Where does your target audience live? For example, are they on Facebook? Is Instagram their destination of choice? Are they active on the conference circuit? Again, this will probably take some testing. And once you invest that time, it will pay you back, because your targeting will be that much more effective.

Finally you want to think of why and how. How will you reach them? What's your strategy? You want to be consistent across every channel you use, which means you have to tailor your content to each. Facebook is going to be a little bit different than Twitter, and

Twitter is going to be a little different than a blog post, but when taken together, each should be coherent parts of the whole of who you are. Having a blog can be useful because it's your personal platform. You have a profile on Twitter, you have a Facebook account, but your blog is really your platform to share your knowledge and go into a little bit more depth than 140 characters or a quick post. Twitter, Facebook, and the others are the distribution system for promoting your blog posts, article shares, and the like. Maybe you've written something on somebody else's site, or somebody that you've been working with has written something that you want to share. That's another way of generating a post, which prompts people to pay attention and gets their followers to know a little bit more about you.

Whatever you're doing, whatever platform you're on, your passion and skill should come across at every level. This applies to your résumé, your online profiles with links to your projects, or any other broadcasting platform. It is especially crucial whenever you're talking with someone on the phone or chatting in person that the passion and the energy you have, the reason why you're doing this, why you're building your brand, should come through. Demonstrate that you have the passion and the desire to carry this through more than just during business hours.

If you're going to be putting all this time and all this energy into branding, you want to do your research and develop a strategy before jumping in. You have to go back to what you want to be and who you want to be.

Informational Interviews

Informational interviews are a good next step after you have done your basic research, and worked to cement your credibility. Doing this in person will let you ask questions in real time, which is vital, as sometimes answers will bring up new questions you might not have thought of otherwise. These informational interviews also help you determine which moves you might want to avoid in your new career.

Of course, one of the best things about informational interviews is that they have the possibility of giving you a tremendous business contact that you can use for years to come. Sounds pretty good, right? The flipside of it is that you actually have to do well in these informational interviews and impress people if you want them to stay in touch with you. Here are some ways that you make that impression.

1. **Be transparent about what you're looking for.**

   Sometimes a friend of a friend asks us to talk to some-body on their behalf to give some career advice. We will gladly do this, but sometimes we meet with somebody and it's hard to tell what exactly they want. Are they looking for background on the industry, how many hours we work, or new contacts for them to follow up with? There are so many different potential agendas that the interviewer might have, that it makes sense for them to be clear about their goals coming out of the meeting. We want to be helpful, so if the interviewer has a directed, specific request, that makes our lives easier. We recommend thinking about what you want to get out of the interview and structuring your questions in order to get the information you need. Even if you're not exactly sure what you want to get out of the interview, do your best to flesh out the reason anyway. You want to appear as targeted as possible, even if, in your own mind, you're still a bit scattered.

2. **Be appreciative that a favor is being done for you.**

   If you're asking a favor of somebody else, do your best to accommodate their schedule. Make sure that it is at a con-venient location for them. They may invite you to their office, but then again, depending on their work circum-stance, they might ask you to coffee. Don't say no to that option just because you don't drink coffee or tea. And def-initely offer to purchase their beverage. It doesn't matter if they make far more money than you do; what matters is that they are taking time out of their busy schedule to spend some time with you. This might seem like a minor detail, but the point is, the interviewee's perception of you will have a significant impact on how enthusiastic and helpful they will be. They might be missing their kids' bedtime tonight because they have to work an hour later after spending an hour to talk to you. A little appreciation goes a long way, and will benefit both parties.

3. **Ask appropriate questions.**

   One thing you should definitely avoid asking, especially up-front, is whether or not your informational interview has a job waiting for you right now. First off, they probably don't; statistically, the odds are very much against that, and if there was a job waiting, you should have figured that out via a search on Google. You don't want to come across as presumptuous, because this person doesn't know you yet and might not be willing to go to bat for you. You're probably putting them in an uncomfortable position.

   However, there are many appropriate questions that you can ask. Find interesting, insightful questions that show that you were listening and very engaged with the conversation. Don't just read from a script; really get to know them, show that you're as interested in getting to know them as you are in furthering your career. Try to find out about what they most enjoy and what they dislike about their job, and the industry in general. Ask what the typical week is like, and what they would change if they could. It's up to your discretion to ask about salary if that would be beneficial to you, but they might not want to discuss particulars with you. However, a broad understanding of salaries can help you determine if you want to go in that direction professionally. Of course, you may be able to find out a general salary range online, which would allow you to forgo potentially uncomfortable questions.

4. **Build your Rolodex.**

   If you keep meeting with good people and they keep introducing you to other good people, you can build your network on an ongoing basis. Although sometimes the interviewee may volunteer recommendations about who to follow up with, that's often not the case. You have to be bold and ask if there's anybody else that it makes sense for you to talk to. As with most requests, the more targeted you are, the better. If you're interested in meeting other people at their company, ask. If you are looking to speak to people who hold a similar job function as your interviewee but at other companies, ask about that.

5. **Keep the relationship.**

   We have both encountered situations where somebody who we gave an informational interview to a few years ago follows up only when they have a request that can benefit their career. They disappear for a while, and show up the moment that they need something. Ask yourself this: If you had a family member or friend who acted in this manner, would it really be an endearing quality? Probably not. The same is true with professional networking. Right after your informational interview, write a follow-up letter thanking them for their time, reminding them nicely about any follow-up that they offered, and from that point on, stay in touch. That doesn't mean writing them every week and hinting about jobs each time. You don't want to put so much pressure on a potential mentor or ally that they start to regret having met you in the first place. It is a good idea to stay in touch maybe every couple of months, adding value to their life. If you read an article that you think would be of interest to them, or you see an opportunity that they could benefit from, send it their way. Nobody wants someone in their life who only wants to take and is never willing to give.

When you are trying to grow your personal brand, it is a good idea to tell these new contacts which skills you're going to be trying to build up with time, and ask for permission to follow up with them for feedback. Get a sense of whether you're going in the right direction.

Leveraging Points of Difference and Transitioning

In order to stand out in your field, you must leverage your points of difference against your competition. For example, there are plenty of political campaigns, especially in primaries, where both of the candidates have positions that are relatively similar. It doesn't really matter how similar the candidates are; what people want to focus on are the differences. In such a situation, candidates are advised to boil down their messages down to the purest form, and focus on what they do better than their opponent. It's not just an art form meant for candidates; homing in on your best talking points is a great way to get prospective employers and partners to understand what you are all about.

One of the most important questions that you need to ask when looking to reinvent yourself is, "What traits do I have that most easily translate into value in a new role or industry?"

Sometimes, the fact that you come from a different industry or professional background can actually be a boon to the company you are trying to join, especially if your particular skills or abilities are in short supply. That's what Jeremy encountered when he was moving from a small, entrepreneurial company—Jurlique—to Kiehl's, a much larger brand owned by L'Oreal. The low-cost, creative entrepreneurial skills that he learned while working for Jurlique were exactly what L'Oreal was looking for at the time. Innovation within the digital marketing space was happening at a breakneck pace in 2009, and L'Oreal, like most multinational conglomerates, had a tendency to move a little slower than the competition. The ability to think outside the box in order to market on a much smaller budget was of interest to L'Oreal, as it meant that Jeremy had the skills to be creative and nimble within this new world.

Sometimes, it's not just one or two related skills and abilities that you have that make you an ideal fit for a new industry; often, it is the combination of a few skills that appear somewhat disjointed at first that make you a major asset to a new field.

Chapter 13

Getting Feedback on Your Personal Brand

Taking Stock

When you're thinking about redefining or reinvigorating your personal brand, the first step is to think about where you stand. Without assessing your current situation, it's impossible to move forward effectively. You have to make sure that you have a reliable read on your brand's value.

You don't necessarily have to put together a focus group to see how effective you are, but you can request peer reviews. Ask for honest feedback on your performance and your value, whether that's from clients, members of your team, or your audience. In some way, shape, or form you should be getting feedback on how you're doing and how your actions correspond to your goal.

For the first step, ask yourself how the world sees you. What do other professionals think of when they think of you? After you exit the party, what did they say about you? If you really investigate, you might be in for some surprises.

If you consider yourself outgoing but most people who you work with consider you to be reserved, you might as well consider yourself to be reserved, too. After all, people probably consider you to be reserved for a reason. Another example is you may intend to come across as humble and eager to learn, but be perceived as nosy. People can't see into your mind; they can only evaluate your actions, and you have to be aware of what those actions mean when others are unaware of your intent. Having a good understanding of the gaps between how you're currently seen and how you want to be perceived is a necessary element in order to work on your personal branding.

Feedback When You're First Starting Out

When you don't have an established presence, it can be tricky or difficult to solicit feedback. Ask friends, family members, and especially mentors and trusted colleagues for their opinions. Keep in mind that it's going to feel very important to get everything exactly right—but if you endlessly polish every last word of your Website, or take two hours to properly construct the perfect tweet, you're going to lose momentum and exhaust yourself. Over-obsession can actually be a detriment. Find a balance between getting your brand right and just getting it out there. You'll refine as you go.

Feedback When You're More Established

After creating a personal brand for yourself, it is crucial to better understand how the rest of the world perceives you. Getting feedback on your personal brand on an ongoing basis is imperative, and having a large audience will help you collect useful data for tracking your progress.

Of course, sometimes anecdotal feedback can be very powerful; just ask Melvin Kearney, the war veteran-turned-actor we met earlier. Melvin thought he would be doing more for people by traveling and meeting with soldiers, which is always going to be a large part of his brand. Still, during his visits with soldiers, he received some surprising feedback. "I've heard from many guys that my acting is actually more inspiring to them," he shares.[1] "One guy told me, 'A lot of guys come home and transition out of the military, and you did those tours gunning. But a lot of guys, we just come home and bury ourselves in a bottle.'" In fact, the U.S. Department of Veterans Affairs released a study in 2013 covering 1999 to 2010 and uncovered that, shockingly, one veteran was committing suicide every 65 minutes. That's 22 every day.

That man Melvin was talking to urges struggling vets to tune in to *Nashville* to catch the vet-turned-actor because "guys can come back from a tour and put on that movie and TV show, and for maybe an hour, you feel back home, and it brings you peace. So be that peace." People reach out to Melvin and tell him that he inspires them by showing that he's doing something with his life.

Proactive Feedback: Surveys

Surveys are an important part of determining how your persona is perceived, so we want to make sure to cover the proper way to conduct them. At some of his previous companies, Jeremy would create an anonymous survey at the start of every new calendar year and distribute it in order to find ways that he could improve during the next year. These questionnaires would go to key vendors, his boss and his boss's boss, people who directly and indirectly reported to him, and colleagues both in his department and other departments whom he had close contact with. Although he kept the results anonymous and didn't know exactly who said what, he did send a slightly different survey to different individuals so that he would know how closely he worked with them. This way he could weigh feedback as more important if it came from somebody who he collaborated more closely with.

Some people don't want to send out a survey, preferring to let others know that this is a serious endeavor by scheduling one-on-one conversations. If you are going to go with this approach, it makes sense to let people know ahead of time the gravity of the interview so that they can treat it with the right degree of sincerity. Also, let them know that they are only one of a select few who you have chosen to be part of this process. People tend to feel honored by things like that and are more likely to take the process seriously. The nice thing about face-to-face interviews is that if somebody says something that you don't quite understand, you can immediately follow up with them for clarification.

The drawback, of course, is that information you received back from people tends to be unstructured or censored. They don't have time to think about how to word their responses or quickly draw on experience, so they might not be able to speak as thoroughly on the topic as you would like. If you send a brief outline of the questions you want to ask ahead of time, you give your respondent a chance to prepare their answers and provide more well-thought-out feedback.

Someone might also hesitate to say something negative to your face. One of the reasons Jeremy prefers electronic communication as a feedback mechanism is because he has a very bad poker face. When people say something that could be somewhat critical with respect to his personal brand, his expression immediately changes. That makes it less likely for the interviewee to continue to be candid throughout the rest of the interview, defeating the purpose. The key to this entire process is to emphasize honesty so that the interviewee is 100 percent comfortable with telling you everything that you need to hear, whether in the short term you will be happy to hear it or not.

Another good idea is to hold a focus group, assuming the people you would like to receive feedback from are nearby. We recommend having five to 10 people in attendance, so keep in mind you have to invite more than that given that some people just won't be able to sync up with your schedule. Simply inform everybody that you're trying to get feedback on your personal brand and you're asking some of your most trusted individuals to give you this honest feedback.

As some people may feel awkward showing up to evaluate one individual, try opening up the floor and make it a round robin discussion. When Ali was ready to make a big professional shift, she joined a career-oriented focus group that met every month. Participants would share their goals and accomplishments, and ask for help evaluating résumé, Website, social media presence, and other important factors. People may be more willing to participate if there's a bit of a give and take. And because your focus group members will want helpful, accurate feedback, they'll have more incentive to be thoughtful in their evaluations.

If you're going to do a focus group, determine who is going to take notes. Depending on the size of your group and your ability to write things down quickly while still helping to facilitate the group, you could possibly do this yourself. However, we recommend getting a friend who is exceptionally strong and detailed when it comes to note-taking in order to write down the key observations generated by the group.

Obviously, a focus group is asking people to leave the comfort of their home and spend time having what may be an awkward discussion with you and some people whom they may not know. However, the people who do show up clearly care about you and are more likely to give you honest and thorough feedback. These individuals are your best source of feedback regarding your strengths and weaknesses.

Because people are helping you, it's a nice idea to give them a small token of appreciation. Maybe provide pizza or drinks if you're meeting in person. Don't give such a large token of appreciation that it seems like you're buying people's impressions, though.

360° Interviews

360° interviews are very important to figuring out what people truly think about you. Many important organizations use this technique in order to get a good sense of how their employees are functioning. You can modify this technique as an individual to get great feedback about how you're doing and if you're actually giving off the personal brand you're trying to convey.

In the 360° review process, your direct supervisor, direct reports, peers, vendors you work with, and so on, will all be encouraged to give honest feedback regarding you and how well you perform at work. The great thing about this process is that you get a sense of how your brand is faring with individuals above, below, and at your level. For example, a lenient boss who might get good feedback from their direct reports may have an offset in the vendors who aren't happy with them because their team might be slow to respond to requests. You can't have a strong personal brand if only your supervisor sees you in the light you want to be seen, or only colleagues in another department see you the way you want to be seen; you want your personal brand to be stable in every possible direction.

You may ask, "How can I get this 360° feedback?" You can encourage your organization to adopt this type of approach to feedback in general. Depending on the size of your organization, it may be untenable to push through a major human resources change, so one alternative would be to hire a corporate coach for yourself to actually speak to people and elicit this type of feedback on your behalf. One thing that we've tried that works well is to send out a survey to everybody we would like to receive 360° feedback from. The one issue with this is that you're the one doing the data collection and people are less likely to believe that it's entirely anonymous. You also should emphasize the seriousness of the review in order to prevent joke answers from skewing your feedback.

If you would like to survey your professional circle to get a sense of where your strengths and weaknesses lie, understand that there is an inherent limitation to this approach. You can stress that the results are 100 percent anonymous, but that may not be enough to elicit purely honest feedback. If you are planning on asking questions yourself, try to ask both positive and negative questions. For instance: "What would you say are my strengths?" should be followed by "What would you say my weaknesses are?" Word your request in such a way that it will attract the most honest feedback. Remember that a close colleague will react differently than a vendor you've only interacted with through e-mail.

Another great way to figure out who you are is to hold informal focus groups of your professional colleagues. It can be uncomfortable to get a group of people together, so approaching these colleagues one at a time will probably be your best bet. If you're unwilling or unable to do focus groups in person, another great option is to examine your digital presence and see what it says about you. It requires more data collection and analysis on your part, but it has the added bonus of keeping the results objective and honest.

If you try to elicit feedback on your own, keep in mind that the types of questions you may want to ask may tip your hand about trying to move away from your current employer. It's very important to look at your questions and then determine how discreet you will have to be. Ask people you have different types of relationships with, including past colleagues, existing coworkers, contacts you know through professional associations, and even friends and family members. Keep in mind who will be the most likely to take the time to give you honest feedback, and choose from a number of groups in order to collect a wide range of opinions.

How *EpicMealTime* Gets Feedback From Their Audience

EpicMealTime is a YouTube cooking show in which the creators cook up monstrosities of meals, racking up the calorie counts with huge amounts of bacon, meat, and booze. But ultimately, *EpicMealTime* is all about the audience. Engaging, teasing, and even taunting their fans, the show has been developed largely based on the response from the viewers.

The amped-up, foul-mouthed Québécois hosts up the ante with every video, displaying calorie counts in excess of 100,000 on screen to boast of their culinary overkill. Started in 2010, the show has had to get creative and adapt as they become more popular and expand to new audiences. You would think that by this point, their shtick would be rather stale, but they keep it fresh because of their heavy use of audience feedback and response.

How they use this feedback, however, is slightly less orthodox than the typical dialogue with their audience. The show is largely ironical and farcical in nature, and the hosts take the same tone with their audience—teasing them, taunting them, and even jokingly calling them out. The main host and voiceover for the show, Harley, addresses all of the imaginary "haters" that are supposedly trash talking the show. The whole thing is over the top and exaggerated, but this ridiculousness also makes viewers feel more comfortable with responding to Harley's taunts, firing back with their own mock insults and reactions, for example: "WHAT DO YOU MEAN NO BACON? WHAT HAVE YOU DONE WITH THE REAL EPICMEALTIME CREW!?!"

For all its mock assaults on the audience, *EpicMealTime* is buoyed by a very strong social media presence. Its hosts promote their Instagram and Twitter accounts heavily, encouraging their audience to talk to them. From tongue-in-cheek retaliatory insults to requests for future meals, the audience participates heavily with the creators of the show, providing an almost endless source of material for future work. In a masterful play, *EpicMealTime* has crowdsourced both its material, while also connecting with their fans. The give and take, the ribbing between the show and its fans, are quite similar to the sort of relationships men of that age and background have with their actual friends, and this makes the audience feel a bond for the show's characters.

Chapter 14

Brand Maintenance: Ongoing Upkeep and Measurement of Your Brand

Keeping your brand fresh, up to date, on target, and true to who you are is a job you'll need to manage for the rest of your life. It's especially important when your career path takes a sudden turn, your experience level and/or abilities shift, or you take on new roles or responsibilities.

The time you spend honing and reinforcing your brand's strengths will yield a significant ROI, so build time for brand maintenance into your schedule just as you would make sure you take time to exercise or practice any other skill. This is non-negotiable!

There are many different practices for keeping your brand vital and thriving. This chapter includes some of our favorites.

Reminders and Appointments

Sometimes, the "Present You" is very devoted to your personal brand development. The problem is, "Future You" may have distractions that get in the way. In other words, your intentions in this moment may outweigh your availability a few days, weeks, months, or even years from now. What's the solution? If you know that Present You is more devoted than Future You, put Present You in the driver's seat.

One of the easier ways to do this is to set up recurring reminders and calendar appointments in order to prevent lapses in concentration or action. This system is very popular—and successful—with people trying to get in good shape. Blocking out time on the calendar for gym appointments is a very effective way to ensure that it actually happens. The same principle is true with respect to getting in good shape professionally.

We've repeatedly heard from professionals who say things like, "I know, I really ought to be on Twitter more often," or "I keep meaning to update my LinkedIn." What's stopping these pros? Procrastination is one factor; an adverse reaction to the concept of professional development is another. Another factor is poor scheduling. If something deserves to be on your calendar, put it on your calendar.

For example, if you're having trouble finding time to develop your LinkedIn profile, put it on your calendar. Depending on your goals, your template may look like this:

- Recurring appointment, every other Sunday, 30 minutes: review your LinkedIn headline and profile.

- Recurring appointment, every Monday and Wednesday, 15 minutes: review your LinkedIn feed for interesting articles to read/share, and comment on connections' activities.

- Recurring appointment, every third Wednesday, 90 minutes: review your recent professional accomplishments to see what can be uploaded to your LinkedIn as a PDF or SlideShare file.

The beauty of a system like this is that it guarantees results. It won't make you an overnight success, but it will give you a baseline of how effective your ongoing maintenance can be. You might find that you're not spending enough time on your recurring brand maintenance appointments. In that case, you can simply change your time allocations. You might find that the appointments you've set are, in hindsight, focused on the wrong activities. That's fine, too: Simply revise your recurring appointments and problem solved. The purpose of recurring appointments is simply to get you moving in the right direction; they should not be static unless and until you are 100 percent sure you've found the optimal setup.

Finding Your Way

When it comes to brand maintenance, one of the best examples we've studied is relationship expert and author Andrea Syrtash, whom we met earlier. Andrea is someone who challenges conventional wisdom: She's in an area of self-help and advice that is often fear-based, but her advice doesn't come from that perspective. She empowers people to take risks.

Andrea was always the advice-giver in her groups of friends and family. "No one I knew from high school is surprised I'm on the track I'm on now," she says with a laugh.[1] In the end, however, it was Andrea's career that chose her, not the other way around. She was a contributor to the 2003/04 book, *How to Survive Dating*, her first time discussing relationships in the media. A publisher invited her to interview hundreds of singles for the book, which was just fine with her, because it was an area of interest. She began to do lots of radio Q&As to support the book, and quickly she discovered that not only did she really enjoy doing them, but people were responding as well.

With the accumulated experience she gained from her interviews, she decided to parlay that knowledge into the arena of matchmaking. In the early 2000s, she put up an ad on Craigslist saying she was interested in editing people's online dating profiles. At this point in time, hysteria around the dangers of online dating was still at a peak, but Andrea saw it as an opportunity for her to put her talents to work. "I was just a writer looking for work," she says. But she quickly realized that her work on dating profiles was filling a real market need.

First things first, Andrea wanted to legitimize her expertise. She went to the Coaches Training Institute, a life coach training program, because she wanted the tools to become a relationship coach. She realized she wanted to do one-on-one and couples coaching, and she knew how important it was to have that sort of formal training. Relationship advice is something many people often feel overconfident about, and she did not want to be cast as an unskilled, unqualified advice giver. If she was going to do this, she was going to do this right.

Once she was certified, she set out to expand her reach. Andrea recalls her desire to reach her audience on multiple platforms. "I realized not everybody will read an article or a book, so TV is important, radio is important.... To me it was multiplatform from the beginning, because I realized I wanted to connect with audiences wherever they were."

She got an offer to be part of a digital series, *Lust for Sex*, in 2006, that never aired because of its racy content, but that led to her getting a chance to host *On Dating*, a digital show, for NBC. Andrea hosted 40 episodes from 2007 to 2009. She caught the attention of Yahoo, which asked her to write a column for them. She was building a brand without even realizing it.

Maintaining a Competitive Edge

Although the addition of new platforms has aided Andrea's growth, it has brought in new challenges as well. "The Internet has opened up a wonderful world of competition. It's exciting to have that," she says. Andrea came through the ranks when the old paradigm was still dominant, when finding outlets for relationship advice required more background in the industry. But she soon found herself competing with bloggers who might have started offering relationship advice on a whim, as opposed to after years of training, and she had to pivot to combat this influx.

Andrea can't just simply make a list of people who aren't qualified to offer advice, of course, and trying to do so would be counter to her mission. "In certain areas, someone will kick my butt, and I've accepted that," she tells us. Instead of trying to push others down, Andrea uses what she has in order to solidify her own brand. For instance, credibility is one reason Andrea has gotten to where she is today. Not everyone can say they have *Oprah* in their bio, or NBC, or TLC. These big brand names give Andrea a little more street cred in an increasingly crowded space, so she builds her brand around that core experience.

She also uses her knowledge of the market in order to gain more of a foothold and tailor her marketing to the audience. She knows what works and what doesn't, and appeals to the clientele she knows so well. Her book titles have spicy names that she knows attract attention: *Cheat On Your Husband (with Your Husband)* is a provocative yet true-to-brand hook. This sort of know-how helps raise her above the less experienced throngs of bloggers.

Living It

Personal branding is about equating yourself with an idea, and that's something that got Andrea to where she is today. She got the NBC gig for *On Dating* simply because she briefly mentioned to Scott Brook, the producer, that she was a writer moving to New York and that she'd like to work with him. It most cases, it would be very likely she'd never hear from him again. But Scott remembered her *four years later*, and e-mailed her as she was en route to New York. That e-mail may seem like a lucky break, but Andrea had planted the seed years before by being proactive and leaving an impression with nothing but her reputation and a few words.

At the end of the day, Andrea is in the business because she feels like it's where she belongs. When asked what she would do if she had to have a 9-to-5 job, Andrea replies, "I have no idea, because this fuels me so much. It's so hard to think about that." Authenticity isn't hard when you believe in your brand and you live it every single day.

The 85 Percent Rule

You need to spend a greater percentage of time refining your brand than actually showcasing it, which is the essence of the 85 percent rule of personal branding.

When building your personal brand, devote 85 percent of your time to behind-the-scenes work; only 15 percent of your time should be for public-facing activities. Like an iceberg, only a small percentage of your personal branding efforts will be visible above water. The 15 percent above the water would include published content such as your articles, as well as any videos, podcasts, status updates, and blog comments. This includes activities such as updating your profile info and networking in person, and one-to-one communications such as e-mail, direct messages, and connecting with people over the phone or in person.

The public-facing content you create is supported by your behind-the-scenes work. When you invest time into absorbing content from articles, books, podcasts, and presentations, the information you glean will be invaluable in helping you to develop your content and strategy. The rule is not a strict one, but it's a good starting guide. It's a reminder that the work nobody sees is just as essential as the articles, blog comments, and everything else that draws attention. Constantly taking in information will help you inform and educate your brand.

If this sounds daunting, keep in mind that there are ways to automate some of the work. You can use listening tools such as Google alerts to collect information, or conduct Twitter searches for relevant material.

Ultimately, keep in mind that a meaningful conversation that occurs behind closed doors can be even more beneficial than 100 tweets cast out into the abyss of the Internet. You'll have to use trial and error to figure out what sort of proportion works for you.

The New Résumé Needs Constant Updating

The standard résumé is quickly becoming obsolete. You have a marketing brochure for brand "you." Instead of your list of titles held and the positions that you've occupied, you have skills that you've mastered, projects that you've delivered, and bragging rights for things that you can genuinely take credit for. And this marketing brochure needs constant updating to reflect the breadth, depth, and growth of your brand.

How do you add to this brochure? First, you need to answer the question of what excites you. Is it learning something new? What's your personal definition of success? Is it money, fame, or doing what you love? Or is it some combination of the three? Search relentlessly for opportunities that fit this mission statement and use those opportunities to develop your skills. Review this mission statement regularly, maybe every six months or so, to make sure you still believe in what you wrote and that the actions that you're taking are helping you to achieve the goals you set out for yourself.

No matter what you're doing, there are four key elements you need to succeed:

- You must have a great teammate and a supportive colleague.
- You must be an expert at something that has actual value.
- You need to be a visionary, a leader, a teacher, and an imaginer.
- You have to be a businessperson.

Know what the pragmatic outcome is and how to get there. It's simple: You are a brand and you're in charge of that brand. There's no single path to success and there's no one right way to create the brand called "you." You just have to start today.

Emma Watson and the Magic of Brand Maintenance

Actress Emma Watson played Hermione Granger from the time she was 11 years old until her early 20s. As she grew up wearing the robes of such an iconic character, many thought she would have trouble moving past that identity. Lauded from the very first movie as the most charismatic and well cast of the three main characters, she cemented herself as an icon in the eyes of her audience. But as Emma grew up and the *Harry Potter* series began to reach its final chapter, it became clear that she wanted more for herself and that she was not content to have the role of Hermione be the defining moment of her life.

Watson was determined to go back to school, and graduated with a degree in English Literature from Brown in May 2014. This was an integral part of returning to normalcy, to branching out into more than acting. Watson often demonstrated a desire to break away from a one-note career, and to not fall prey to the sort of destructive pattern that so many child stars have followed.

For Watson, the question of the next step became clear, as she developed an interest in social justice. Having been the object of leering fascination before she was even an adult, Emma was determined to work against the issues she encountered in her own life. She has advocated for women's education and their political participation, and worked to reverse perceptions of feminism as "man-hating."

Her efforts have done as much for her own image as they have for feminism. But why has she been able to move on whereas other child stars have struggled? The key to Emma's success is her escalation. She stepped onto a bigger stage. It's hard to keep an even keel and stay the course after an undertaking as big as the *Harry Potter* franchise. It's almost a minor form of depression; when everything stops, what do you do?

Emma's appointment as a UN Women Goodwill Ambassador and her HeForShe campaign were a step up from her acting, put her in the public eye in a very present way, and gave her something to strive for. By leveraging her fame, she turned it into a tool rather than her defining characteristic.

Ongoing Measurement

It's helpful to approach your branding efforts objectively, even scientifically. The best way to keep track of the results of each action is to:

- ✤ Create an objective for yourself.
- ✤ Measure success in a way that tells you something about the quality of your methods.

If you don't define your goals, how will you know if you're succeeding? Set targets to aim for in the process of building your brand. If you don't know what you're trying to accomplish, there's only a small chance that you will be successful.

Use this outline of clear goals, with specific and quantifiable measures, to determine whether or not your efforts are actually paying off. In doing so, you will be better able to hold yourself accountable. If you have a clear idea of what you're supposed to be accomplishing, it will be easier to see when you need to make adjustments.

Tracking less quantifiable measurements—such as goodwill toward your brand—are tougher, but you can use statistics such as the number of times someone mentions your brand in a positive manner as a proxy measure.

Make sure to develop key performance indicators (KPIs) for your program, statistical measures that help you track your campaign's overall effectiveness at reaching the targets that you established at the outset. Your KPIs have to be linked directly to your goals.

One KPI we would recommend focusing on is your brand's Conversational Reach, which is simply the average number of replies or comments per post. The engagement that your brand generates on Facebook is a major component of Facebook's algorithm for determining the odds that your brand posts will be displayed in a fan's feed.

Content Amplification is another very useful KPI because it indicates the number of shares, retweets, and Google +1s per brand post. Shares are implied endorsements and allow your message to extend way beyond your current network.

Adam Cohen: Always Evolving

Adam Cohen of *DaDa Rocks* consistently goes back to his brand to revaluate it. "I've had to consider what my direction is and what platforms I'm going to be broadcasting from, how the look and feel fits or has to change to fit the medium."[2] And as the platforms themselves evolve, the brand has to evolve with it. As Facebook, Twitter, Instagram, and others add or modify existing options, there is a need to stay on top of the changes in order to give the impression of a matching brand evolution. "You constantly have to look at yourself and say, is this the right path; is this the right direction? And if you make the wrong decision, you have to be prepared to work with the result and see what you can do better."

Your Digital Footprint

In an ideal world, your digital presence is already pitch perfect. It only includes amazing, insightful, positive quotations from very reputable publications, and glowing recommendations from industry leaders. The more likely scenario is that you have a few good things posted about you online, but also a decent amount of content that doesn't reflect the brand you're trying to put out there. If you are a stockbroker now but you were an award-winning high school basketball player a decade ago, those results might dominate your Google results. You also might have a problem if you have a relatively popular name. You might think that there aren't that many Jeremy Goldmans, but Goldman is incredibly common among Jewish people—our version of the surname Smith—and Goldmans love to name their sons Jeremy. So there are a number of Jeremy Goldmans out there, making it a little bit trickier for Jeremy to Google himself.

There are also plenty of Google results that you might not want to associate with your brand. You might have had a difficult breakup with someone who then posted negative things about you on Facebook or Twitter. Long ago, Jeremy had written some *LiveJournal* posts professing his love for an ex, which showed up when you Googled his name. Even though the content may be ancient history, the continued existence of digital information stands as an example of why you have to be careful about what you write and what your privacy settings are.

When it comes to privacy settings, many people immediately think about Facebook. Although you definitely want to be careful about what is public and what is not on Facebook, it's a pretty big Internet out there, and there are many other corners that you want to scrub clean. It's important to see what shows up when you look for yourself on other sites, even those you wouldn't immediately associate with your online persona. One executive that we know, believe it or not, had the bright idea of posting a picture of himself along with his real first name on Craigslist—in the "casual encounters" section. Oh, and he was married. Not the kind of thing that's going to do wonders for your reputation.

When Jeremy was younger, he used to be an active participant in a number of Yahoo! Groups. Sometimes, not even posting something but simply being a member of a group with an inappropriate name can reflect poorly on your personal brand. That's not to say you should stop being yourself: It's okay to be an individual. You just have to understand that, for better or for worse, what you say might be taken out of context by potential employers and business partners before they even have a chance to really get to know you.

A significant part of your personal brand is formed based on your digital presence. Though your colleagues generate their perceptions of you based on face-to-face and over the phone interactions, there will be content about you that influences popular opinion. You don't have to be that famous to have plenty written about you at various sites and platforms. You need to conduct a thorough review and come up with a strategy to control your digital persona.

Step one is to Google yourself. Because that is exactly what potential employers or clients are going to do when considering whether to work with you. Make sure to write your name in quotes to get accurate results. Another good idea is to subtract the relevant terms. There is a Jeremy Goldman in Orange County who's a criminal defense attorney. Jeremy puts the minus symbol directly before "Orange County" in a search in order to filter out these results. Finally, make sure to check page two! Even if you haven't gone past page one in the last half decade, you may still find some references to yourself buried deep in the bowels of the Internet.

Kanye Controls His Brand

Rapper, producer, fashioner designer—Kanye West is many things, but he's not an idiot. He might not be the nicest guy, but don't let that fool you into thinking that his antics are as asinine as they appear to be on first glance. Can being a jerk be a useful personal brand? Absolutely, if you play it right. We usually think of personal branding in terms of positive characteristics—intelligence, talent, creativity. But negative publicity can be almost as useful as positive publicity. "No news is good news" does not apply when you're as popular as Kanye. All press is good press.

A few times a year, Kanye has an incident like interrupting Taylor Swift as she accepted her VMA award; things that seem like a joke, until he takes it another step further. He's developed a pattern: Once the incident passes, he barely comments, lets the social media buzz about his antics reach a fever pitch, and goes back to focusing on his music. Kanye barely refers to these incidents after the fact, occasionally apologizing soon after. In doing so, he mitigates the negative effects of his actions without losing his place in the news. He exploits free media attention for exposure, and solidifies his brand in the process.

Kanye does not just exploit the news, but also that most irrevocable law of personal branding: Whatever you want to be known for, be great at it. He's confident enough in his abilities (obviously) that people admit, "Yeah, he's kind of a jerk, but I can't stop listening to his music." At the end of the day, Kanye is in a profession where people can separate him from his product when necessary. As long as people enjoy his music, they will listen to it even if they don't like him, in the same way that people will continue to shop at stores that reportedly underpay employees. You might not like how those businesses operate, but the corporation provides a service useful or enjoyable enough to outweigh your reservations.

Outside of raw publicity, Kanye has also created a character that forms the basis of much of his music. He's a "bad boy." If you listen to his lyrics, you'll notice that they often mirror his personal life: It's a constant battle of ups and downs, mistakes and apologies, self-condemnation and redemption.

But don't Kanye's antics alienate some of his fan base? Not if sales and praise are any indication. The people who are going to listen to his music are not put off, and the people who don't like him are not the ones who are going to listen to him anyway. And given the way other notorious celebrities behave, Kanye is far from the limits of what you can get away with when you're rich and popular.

Chapter 15

Becoming Awesome

Organizing Your Branding Strategy

"I'll start my personal branding project first thing tomorrow, promise." Does that sound like something you'd say? Probably everyone can relate, so maybe it's a good idea to talk about procrastination, and why we tend to fall prey to it. Let's face it: We all procrastinate every now and then. The excuses vary from "too busy" to "not the right time" and so on, particularly with the more important, time-consuming projects, such as developing a personal branding statement. We continue to rationalize the delays to the point where we start to believe just about any excuse we give ourselves.

"Some contingencies are especially seductive," says Bill Knaus, EdD, coauthor of *Overcoming Procrastination*. "Thinking you have to feel motivated to do something that you are not motivated to do usually means that you'll lose time waiting for motivation to magically appear."[1]

"Procrastinators actively look for distractions, particularly ones that don't take a lot of commitment on their part," according to Hara Estroff Marano, *Psychology Today* editor at large.[2]

So, what's really holding you back from being productive and accomplishing what you set out to do? The answer is simple: fear—the fear of taking a risk and failing, the fear of looking foolish and wounding your pride.

As time passes, our fear often grows and can become so overwhelming that we may give up entirely. Here are three steps to loosen the grip of procrastination and actively jump into the world of personal branding:

1. **Give yourself a deadline.**

   Write down what you want to achieve and set a deadline. Don't grant yourself any extensions, either. Place this note in a location where you can always see it. And both tangible (for example, a Post-it) and intangible digital reminders are helpful. We use Asana to schedule tasks and sync them to our Google Calendars, so we'll have reminders of upcoming tasks wherever we go.

2. **Start small.**

   It's normal to get swept up in the overwhelming feelings that come along with a big project or goal. The most effective way to combat this is to break down your goal into small steps. When you're trying to be productive, don't think in terms of projects; think in terms of specific tasks. This will keep you on track and help you stay positive in the process. And you can check off the intermediate steps as you go, which is both satisfying and helps you feel like you're making constant progress.

3. **Create rewards for success and consequences for failure.**

   As you complete each step, motivate yourself to keep going: Positive reinforcement provides incentive and will make you feel good about yourself. Likewise, *don't* reward yourself for not following through. Be a fair but stern boss to yourself.

Today is a perfect day to start cutting down on procrastination. Take five minutes now to think of a few tasks you've been putting off and make a plan for tackling them. Do it now. Don't procrastinate.

Time Management

The prospect of working as a freelancer is exciting and freeing, and it appeals to our entrepreneurial spirit. The idea of making your own hours, doing what you want, and doing work on your own terms seems ideal. But it's important to remember some of the more challenging aspects of freelance work—namely, that finding the right balance is tougher than you might think. You are responsible both for marketing and for taking care of business duties, and making everything work requires a substantial amount of planning.

When working to establish your brand, it is important to remember that everything you're doing is your job. You need to schedule time each day to work. There are two sides to your business: delivering services to clients, and doing your marketing work. As the old TV ad asked, "Is running your business getting in the way of running your business?"

Split up your day into concrete chunks. The specifics of this process are up to you, so go with what makes the most sense for your working style. For instance, you might spend the morning completing projects for clients and the afternoon or a few hours in the evening on marketing tasks like social networking. Or, take an afternoon nap and do the bulk of your work late at night. Do what works for you. But no matter your preference, consistency is key. Having a daily schedule keeps you on task, and having specific goals to hit ensures that you spend your time wisely.

Your schedule should include not only the hours you plan to work, but also the tasks you want to accomplish each day. Because you're not getting paid by the hour, each one becomes either an opportunity or a waste. Self-employment gives you the chance to shape the nature and direction of your career, as well as your personal brand. But in order to be successful and reach your goals, it is imperative that you manage your time wisely, focus on tasks that generate income, and actively work to minimize interruptions.

Setting a Social Marketing Schedule

Marketing takes time and energy, so it always surprises us when we see people fail to factor in the investment to determine strategy, choose the content their brand is interested in creating, and so forth. Engaging with your audience is time-consuming; the actual day-to-day interactions take up a significant amount of time by themselves, and that's not including time you'll have to spend deciding what to talk about, which topics to blog on, and finding media to add to your social presence.

The best way to organize your time and increase your efficiency is to set a social media schedule and stick to it. That includes time for brainstorming ideas for new content and deciding when to post it. Depending on your needs and preferences, you can organize this any way you like. But leaving tasks open-ended is a surefire way to waste time. You have to set deadlines for yourself, and having a strict schedule will keep you focused.

Although each second is precious, there are some times when you have to put in big investments in order to develop your brand. For instance, your social marketing efforts can hinge on your knowledge of your audience's identity and what they'll be interested in. This may include tracking the click-through rate (CTR) from social networks to your blog, and then analyzing the types of topics that are most likely to get clicked on and most likely to be shared. From that, you can get a sense of what your audience is interested in.

How to Make Every Day Exceptionally Productive

Sometimes you can get stuck in the grind for too long, and need to break yourself out of a rut. You're exhausted and can't get anyone on the phone, and the days just seem to get away from you. If you need to make a commitment to make today—and every day—one of the most productive days of the week, not the least, here are some ways to make the time stand out:

1. **Start your workday** *earlier* **in the day than usual.**

   This might be counterintuitive if you're struggling with fatigue, but hear us out. Right now your energy might be waning, but starting early gets you in the right mindset for the day—you're on a mission to make today productive before it even begins. The key is to go to bed especially early the night before so you can start an hour earlier than usual and not need to hit the snooze button.

2. **Don't check your e-mail for the first two hours of the day.**

   Even if you went to bed earlier, there's a good chance your energy will dwindle through the course of the day. Given that, don't waste your peak hours at the start of the day on e-mail. You can even use a tool such as StayFocusd or Block Site to block your access to your Webmail during certain hours to help you stay focused.

3. **Work on a major initiative you've been putting off.**

   If you're already struggling to get out of a rut, you may find that even though you're rushing around to get back on the right track, nothing of major substance is happening. You're in such a hurry to be productive that you're avoiding the most time-consuming and dreaded tasks. Instead of trying to multitask, block out one or two at the beginning of every day. That way, even if you get a sudden bout of food poisoning at your lunch break and your workday ends suddenly, it's already been a very productive day (we suggest not getting food poisoning, though, as it's not the kind of productivity that will help your brand).

4. **Don't send e-mails; schedule them.**

   Don't be in such a rush to do things *now* that you sacrifice
   good timing for the feeling of productivity. For instance,
   Jeremy has done data analysis to show that Friday is the
   worst day to e-mail people, assuming you actually want
   a response. Instead, he writes e-mails but schedules them
   to get sent later. Two of his favorite tools for doing this
   are Boomerang for Gmail and Sidekick from HubSpot.
   Jeremy tries to schedule e-mails for Monday afternoon or
   Tuesday morning, rather than first thing Monday morning (or anytime on a Friday, when most people's minds are
   already out the door).

5. **Plan the week ahead carefully.**

   Look over your calendar to make sure you're fully prepared for any upcoming meetings. Sometimes, Ali's Friday
   review of next week's meetings will uncover that she has
   lunch appointments with two different clients at the same
   time, which is never a good thing. Also, sometimes she'll
   notice awkward gaps between two presentations in a certain region, which is a prompt for her to visit LinkedIn
   to see if anyone from her network is nearby. It's nice to be
   able to use that down time to catch up with a connection—
   or even meet them face-to-face for the first time.

These are our secrets to getting the week back on track. Adopt a
few of these, and there's a good chance you'll head into Friday night
feeling like you're entitled to a great, relaxing weekend.

Getting Organized—but Not Too Organized!

While planning is useful, you should also remember to set aside
time to be flexible. You don't want to overlook or be unable to take
advantage of unexpected opportunities. The more structured your
schedule, the less you're able to mold to extraneous circumstances.
Staying flexible is key, so that when you encounter some unexpected

event (good or bad), you can roll with it, and even make it a part of your social marketing strategy.

Marketing Automation

Automation is incredibly useful, as it allows you to spend more time on high-value work and less time on tedious tasks. However, poorly planned automation can diminish the social interaction with your fans and turn them off your brand entirely.

One example of good automation is using a tool to simplify or automate posting your long-form (that is, blog) content to Facebook, Twitter, and other social platforms. One of our favorite tools is called IFTTT, which stands for "if {this} then {that}." IFTTT simply lets users stitch together all their digital properties so that *if this* particular event occurs, *then* do *that* (something else) in response.

You can then connect IFTTT to Buffer, a tool that lets you optimize all your brand's sharing across its social platforms. We've mentioned Buffer in previous chapters, but it's especially relevant here; Buffer gives you an easy interface to schedule when you'll be sharing the great content that you find on the Web, as well as any of your own content that you wish to share.

However, there is a trade-off to automation: When you post a link to a blog post yourself, you are able to craft the perfect lead-in and context for a link, things which typically bring your brand more likes, comments, and retweets.

Making Personal Branding More Enjoyable

We all have good days and bad days at work. Jeremy and Ali both feel fortunate that their work is both interesting and fulfilling (most days, anyway). But what's the key to overall happiness in the workplace? The good news is that creating a positive work environment is actually quite simple, and involves a few small shifts that can make a major difference. Here are five ways to improve your outlook and productivity:

1. **Give yourself something to work toward.**

    When you're working on your personal brand, you will probably have days when you're feeling tired, frustrated, and discouraged. Remember that the whole process is continuous. It's about constant improvement and maintenance, so there isn't really a point when it's "finished." If you don't have an endpoint, the whole thing can feel like a Sisyphean task. But normal businesses are never "finished" either (if they're lucky). How do they keep their employees happy? They do so with projects, goals, and milestones. Give yourself things to accomplish in finite amounts of time, and give yourself rewards when you reach those goals. You need something to work toward in the short term or you can get burnt out. But even when you have smaller tasks to accomplish, keep in mind that you're running an endurance race, not a sprint. Don't burn yourself out in the first mile.

2. **Make things easy for yourself.**

    Ali makes time to go to the gym several days a week. Depending on her schedule, sometimes that means she has to train early in the morning. To help her get going, she either sleeps in her activewear (which are basically like high-tech pajamas anyway) or picks out her clothes for both workout and work the night before. She fills a bottle of water and leaves it in the fridge, and gets her coffee and breakfast all set up. Ali makes things easy for herself, because if at any point during the process she hits an obstacle, it can derail the whole process.

    Jeremy does the same thing for himself at work: He makes it easy. Doing the little things and avoiding the small frustrations that build up during the day can be crucial during times of stress. Do you ever have those long days where your papers blow away in the wind, or you spill your entire cup of coffee on yourself, or your computer crashes in the middle of a 10-page document? When you say, "Okay, you win, I'm going back to bed"? Eliminating the possibility of setbacks can be a big help at the start of a long week, and can go a long way toward helping you avoid adding anything to the day's frustrations.

3. **Help your team.**

Regardless of how busy you are, if a colleague or an employee asks for assistance on a project, there's a good chance you'll get a jolt of happiness out of agreeing to help. And they'll feel better about being on the same team with you. According to a study by Donald Moynihan and Kohei Enami of the University of Wisconsin-Madison and Thomas DeLeire of Georgetown University, going out of your way to help others in the workplace can increase personal happiness.[3]

4. **Make time to socialize.**

Though it's important not to overshare with your coworkers, you should show an interest in their personal life. Even a brief "How was your weekend?" can make a major difference.

"Socializing with your coworkers is essential for your career," says Alexander Kjerulf, the founder of Woohoo Inc. and one of the world's leading experts on happiness at work. "If you're not able to relate to your coworkers as human beings and build positive relationships, your career will suffer."[4]

Getting to know your fellow employees as people will help you to communicate better, trust each other more, and collaborate better. In turn, this will make you happier and more productive in general.

5. **Find meaning in your work.**

Research from the University of Warwick suggests that happiness makes people 12 percent more productive.[5] The key between happiness and productivity is undeniable. Even if your current job isn't a perfect fit, you can always reframe your perspective to see how you are positively contributing. Keep a log of every day's "greatest hits" at work to find meaning and value in what you're doing.

"When you engage in activities that are meaningful to you, you'll feel more inspired, satisfied, motivated—and happy," according to an infographic from Happify on maximizing happiness in the workplace.[6]

How to Say No Without Sounding Negative

Are you a people pleaser? Do you consider yourself the type of person who says yes to everything? (Did you answer yes to these two questions, too? Jeez, it's worse than we thought.) It's normal to feel uncomfortable saying no to a boss, supervisor, or client, but there are ways to turn someone down while still maintaining a healthy and respectful relationship. The secret largely lies in giving a positive, constructive response when responding in the negative.

Jeremy doesn't always say no at work. But he used to be way worse. He would say yes more often than just about anyone he knew. He was so dead-set on being highly successful at a young age that his default answer was yes. In fact, he sometimes would say yes before being asked to do something. He would volunteer for assignments that he wasn't the most qualified for, all in an attempt to prove himself.

What Jeremy didn't know earlier in his career, when he was saying yes to just about any request made of him, is that it's possible to say no in a way that builds a relationship, rather than tearing it down. If you turn down an assignment, it's important to thoroughly explain your reasons for doing so and then offer an alternative. If you present your argument in a diplomatic yet direct way, your boss will likely be less defensive and more open to hearing what you have to say.

Greg McKeown illustrates this point perfectly in his bestselling book *Essentialism*. When your boss asks you to tackle a new project, McKeown recommends asking which of your other assignments can be put to the side so that you will have enough time to devote to the new task. The beauty of this strategy is that you're getting your point across without actually saying no.

"At every meeting you have, ask what is its one key purpose—the one thing you want to have happen as a result. If there isn't one, then don't have the meeting," McKeown says. "And if there is, then fight for that one thing in the meeting. And when you have got it, end the meeting."[7]

To Gaby Dalkin of *What's Gaby Cooking*, staying on brand and keeping relevancy in mind can help her make those tough calls to say no. She always thinks about what her audience wants to see from her. For example, she knows that if she were to put something up on Instagram, and it's not true to the *What's Gaby Cooking* brand, it's not going to perform well. With that in mind, learning how to say no became a crucial part of her growth, as it helped her to better define her brand. "When I say no to working with a different brand, or some sort of sponsored content because it's not true to who I am, I think everyone who follows me—whether it's on the blog or some other social channel—appreciates that they're getting an authentic version of me. I have to really pay attention to what I'm doing."[8]

Gaby's "secret sauce" on those platforms is to consistently figure out what works the best for her brand and focus on those efforts. For the past year, Gaby has focused on improving her Instagram content, which has been growing dramatically as a result. She is constantly analyzing the feedback she receives from specific posts to understand what her audience wants to see.

Whether it's at work or at home, there are consequences to taking on more than you can handle. The more we try to juggle, the less focused and productive we become overall. In some cases, it's in your best interest to be accommodating. And if it's a project you're genuinely excited about, find out if the deadline is flexible or if you can reprioritize other work. But other times it makes more sense to politely decline. The trick—and it's not always easy—is learning to tell the difference.

It's okay to say no when:

There's not enough time. Be realistic if there aren't enough hours in the day—or week—to finish the assignment. If you're not sure if you have enough time, try to estimate how long it will take to complete everything on your plate already. When in doubt, add some cushion, as we've found many things take more time than you initially expected. A good solution is to offer a timeline that works for *you*. This works in two ways: it demonstrates exactly how busy you are, and it also makes the person giving you work reevaluate whether or not you should be the person to give it to. It's more concrete than "I can't do this right now," and lets them know that you're willing, but just not available.

The rest of your work will suffer. Will taking on another project prevent you from giving other tasks the proper time and attention? Don't put yourself in the position of missing a deadline or doing a rushed job. If you botch a task you had previously agreed to, no one's going to focus on that extra job you just said yes to—they're going to focus on the one you screwed up.

You don't feel qualified. If you don't feel confident that you have the skills to do what's being asked of you, it's in your best interest to say so. In this situation, your boss might reply, "I wouldn't give this to you if I thought you couldn't handle it." To support your stance, make a list of resources you would need in order to feel comfortable taking on the project.

The company itself will suffer. At times, you'll be asked to do something that you know will put the company in worse financial shape, even if your boss doesn't yet realize it. It's a difficult situation to be in, but you have to be prepared to suggest the counterpoint in a non-threatening way. Let the other party reconsider their initial request; if you don't come off as too strident in your argument, you might just win them over and win some respect in the process.

If you're having trouble saying no, think back. Have there been other times when you said no to your boss? How did it turn out? What would you do differently next time? What if you are the boss? How do you feel about your direct reports saying no to you? Do you expect your employees or team to follow every order, or do you encourage debate and discussion?

Making Harder Decisions Can Lead to Success

Jeremy was at his favorite Cleveland sandwich shop, Melt, while visiting his in-laws, and ordered two immense sandwiches. Seriously, those things are *huge*. Jeremy's proud of his determination, but he was having trouble finishing the second sandwich. It was disappointing, because he first discovered Melt on the TV show *Man v. Food*, in which host Adam Richman chowed down on immense meals on a routine basis.

It would have been difficult for Jeremy to finish the second sandwich, but it was possible. What was even more difficult for him in this situation, however, was to quit. After fighting it for a few more minutes—and taking a few more bites—he realized that he had to quit, precisely because, for him, *that* was the greater challenge.

When you're debating between two courses of action, it pays to listen to your gut. At the same time, it also pays to think about what will be more difficult for you. Life isn't easy. Think about it: If the path of least resistance were consistently the right choice, wouldn't everyone take it? If it were very easy to build a social network with hundreds of millions of users, wouldn't more people do it? If it were a cinch to innovate in the search category to take users away from Google, wouldn't all competitors be compelled to do it? If everyone gets drawn to the same honey pot, doesn't the pot eventually run out of honey?

And though honey may be sweet, pushing yourself past where you *thought* your boundaries were is even sweeter. It's a great feeling to tackle the path of greater resistance and realize you're a tougher individual afterward.

For Jeremy, "Do the hard thing" extends not just to putting down sandwiches, but business challenges as well. Take networking, for example. Jeremy's network probably considers him to be a major extrovert. After all, he's built a company that focuses on digital communications. He started a 300-strong networking group, Mosaic, based out of New York. Jeremy also consciously decided to acquire five pets, a spouse, and a kid.

At the same time, in many ways he's quite introverted. There was a time when going to a networking event, especially without a wingman, was terrifying to him. It was so terrifying, in fact, that he simply never did it. Yet Jeremy fought against his instinct to avoid doing the hard thing—forcing himself to come out of his shell—and he couldn't be happier about that decision.

Some people are cynical and will take this advice to the point of absurdity. Of course you shouldn't go out of your way to invent stupid challenges for yourself. When you're at a crosswalk and you don't have the light, don't close your eyes and just start walking across the street. When you're launching a business that you project will require $20 million in startup capital, don't try to bootstrap it yourself just because that will be harder. Harder doesn't have to equal hardheaded.

We're merely advocating taking the harder path when you're truly torn between two forks in the road. And by consistently taking the harder path, you'll toughen yourself with time. That's what we want for you. It might be counterintuitive, but if anything, common sense is anything but common. Embrace the harder path often enough, and eventually you'll find that each time you do it, it's not that difficult. You'll get used to consistently challenging yourself, whether it's writing a business plan, firing a consultant who just isn't working out, or simply allowing yourself *not* to finish that second sandwich.

On Branching Out

Being an entrepreneur requires knowledge—even of topics that aren't exactly in your job description. Because when you're an entrepreneur, everything is in your job description. So although you might not be a financial expert, you should acquaint yourself with some basics to make sure you can understand the numbers and make a useful economic model.

Just ask entrepreneur extraordinaire Nolan Bushnell, who founded Atari and Chuck E. Cheese's (his opinions are more than worth their weight in arcade tokens). The biggest failing Bushnell has identified in entrepreneurs is the inability to understand the financial and practical underpinnings of their ideas.

If an entrepreneur says, "Well, I don't do spreadsheets," or "I'm not a finance guy," that's the wrong answer for Bushnell. In his eyes, "The person who runs the company has to be the chief architect and has to have a financial plan for their idea, or it is a nonstarter."[9]

10 Ways to Unplug and Become More Productive

Many of us are busy, digitally savvy professionals obsessed with productivity. The problem is digital savvy and productivity do not always go hand in hand.

For those of us who want to promote more balance in their lives—while still being plugged in a good chunk of the time—there are a few easy and quick changes that will make a huge difference. Jess Davis, founder of Folk Rebellion (a boutique lifestyle brand celebrating unplugging and striking the proper life balance), is someone people routinely come to for unplugging advice.

Here are Davis's expert tips for how to gain a huge productivity boost:

1. **Start the day off right.**

    "Mornings should be sacred alone time for your brain," says Jess.[10] Remove the cell phone from beside your bed. If your phone serves as your alarm clock, purchase an inexpensive alarm clock. Start your day without Kardashian-related breaking news phone notifications infiltrating your brain. Use this time to set your goals for the day. Without unnecessary phone distractions, you might even be able to start work earlier.

2. Prioritize e-mails.

Jess advises everyone to handle your most important e-mails first, and whenever possible, batch e-mails together. For example, rather than bouncing between e-mails pertaining to 15 different projects, use keyword searches and filters to focus on one project at a time. Your brain will spend less time switching between tasks, which will let you unplug faster.

3. Encourage phone calls.

Manage people's expectations about when to hear back from you via e-mail. If they don't expect a response as quickly, they will be less likely to freak out and send multiple e-mails. Jess's e-mail signature explicitly encourages phone calls if she is needed urgently.

4. Get your device off your person.

Try not to have your phone in your pocket or within arm's reach at all times. "As an addict myself, I notice that if it's easy to reach, I check it," says Jess. To conquer this, she recommends putting some physical distance between yourself and your device. For focus, stow it away it in a desk drawer while working on a deadline that requires your undivided attention.

5. Social? Think desktop.

Although many of us think of phones as productivity devices, the reality is we often use them for less focused purposes. Jess recommends not checking social media on the fly; rather, consider consuming it on a desktop. Between faster Internet connections and speedier typing, you can get through your social media to-do list faster if it's on a desktop.

6. Lunchtime means break time.

"Take your lunch away from a screen," advises Jess. "Even if it's 15 minutes. Walk without your phone. I promise the world will not explode if you are unavailable for less than an hour."

7. **Always on = less productive.**

   Studies are consistently proving that the "always on" mentality leads to diminished productivity. "When you leave work, leave work," says Davis, as those who do not unplug to some extent tend to burn out. "I am sure there will be people in your life happy to see your face without the glow from your screen."

8. **Tangible isn't a bad thing.**

   When possible, replace screens with tangible objects such as books or magazines, which help train your brain to read long form and may improve focus. Furthermore, short digestible online content forces you to click to more content more frequently, costing you precious seconds of lost productivity. Which, over time, adds up.

9. **Use your hands.**

   In her research, Jess has found that people who do things with their hands for a living or have hobbies involving their hands are less "addicted" to technology. She hypothesizes it's because their hands are always busy. "Musicians, makers, artists, dancers, athletes, yogis, surfers all are less tethered because they have something in their life where either a phone can't enter or their hands are too busy to be bothered." You might not be cut out to be a yogi, but a hobby to keep your hands occupied might help you unplug.

10. **Bring manners back.**

   Be courteous and put the phone away for meetings, meals, and while being waited on either at a coffee shop, takeout counter, or restaurant. Plain and simple, it's rude not to. You may think you're being more productive, but you'll get through the checkout faster if you're not distracted. At business functions, you may even meet a key new contact or close an important deal, all because you were unplugged and focused on the humans around you. And the humans around you are, ultimately, the people you're trying to reach through building your personal brand.

Conclusion

Congrats—you finished *Getting to Like*! (Or maybe you're the type of person who skips to the end; we won't judge, but the next few pages might not make too much sense yet. It's your call.)

We hope that what you've read has been helpful. You should feel prepared to take what you've learned, or at least a few tips that resonated with you the most, and apply those to your brand and your strategy. Let's do a quick review:

Maybe you started at the very beginning and worked on developing an attention-getting brand statement, then built that out into a compelling narrative. Or perhaps you buckled down and started creating a bank of content in your chosen media format—blog posts, podcasts, videos, images, or a combination thereof.

No matter your preferred type(s) of content, we hope you experimented with finding the digital platforms that work best for you. At minimum, you should have a Website and a presence on at least one type of social network. Your LinkedIn profile should be look-ing pretty appealing by now; don't forget to update that regularly. We bet your Twitter feed is humming (chirping?) with activity. Just remember to translate your digital attempts into in-person network-ing activities, too. Go to conferences. Meet people. Make friends and connections that you'd never find if you didn't leave the digital space once in a while—and then use those social channels to stay connected with them.

While you're at it, give yourself a quick reality check. Are you presenting a too-idealized version of yourself, or have you gotten comfortable with your quirks and idiosyncrasies so that you can have meaningful connections with your audience? If you have mul-tiple facets of your identity to reconcile, have you found a way to make these different aspects of your personality help you stand out in a positive way?

With any luck, you've avoided running into any personal brand-ing disasters. But, if you have made a blunder, we hope you've recov-ered well and have learned from the experience. Or maybe you've realized that what your brand needed was a partial (or total) over-haul. Either way, make sure you ask some trusted sources for feed-back as you move forward. As you're incorporating their sugges-tions and advice, take the time to do a little spring cleaning around your digital persona.

It might be too soon to maintain the brand you just established (or reinforced), but it's never too soon to plan for that upkeep. Remember to set some calendar reminders so that you can continue to keep testing, refining, tweaking, and perfecting. Get comfortable making updates and doing all that behind-the-scenes work, because that's not going away any time soon.

Finally, we hope you're taking all those time management and anti-procrastination tips from the previous chapter (what do you mean, you'll read it tomorrow?) and applying them to everything else you've learned. We wrote that chapter specifically to support and reinforce all the other advice we included leading up to that point; although we won't say it's the most important chapter, the information there is useful no matter what other advice of ours you choose to follow.

So Now What?

We'd love to leave you with a reassuring promise that from here on out, you'll be all set. Clients and partners will flood your inbox with offers. You'll have a perfect, timeless, bulletproof brand that you'll never have to worry about again.

Well, if you're smart enough to invest in *Getting to Like*, you're already wise enough to know that's not true.

We can't make any predictions, but we can make one guarantee: The world is going to continue to change. And would you really want the workplace, the economy, and humanity in general to stand still? They will continue to evolve, and that's not a bad thing. New trends will take the place of what's currently en vogue, new social channels will rise, and others may become less useful. You'll always be adjusting.

But the good news is that if you follow the principles we've laid out here, you're going to be able to evolve, too. You'll be adding more skills, growing your network, and making yourself more attractive to prospective contacts. Instead of dreading change, you'll be ready for it. And you'll be more prepared than those (read: your peers and your competition) who aren't anticipating or even looking forward to the next big thing.

With the right mindset and a little diligence, you can stay ahead of the curve. You might even be the next trendsetter who people watch, follow, and emulate. So figure out which social channels work for you. Continue to share your unique voice and perspective. Keep making contacts and maintaining those connections, both digitally and in real life. If you can find what excites you and find a way to do that every day, then you have a bright future ahead of you—and we're proud of you for investing the time and effort in your brand.

And remember, if at any time you feel stuck, confused, over-whelmed, stressed, or even just hungry, use #GtoL to reach out to us. We'll be there with advice, answers, or some pretty awesome sandwich ideas—whatever you need.

Thanks for reading!

Jeremy and Ali

May 2016

Notes

Chapter 1

1. David K. Williams, "10 Reasons to Stay at a Job for 10 or More Years," Forbes.com, *www.forbes.com/sites/davidkwilliams/2012/09/29/10-reasons-to-stay-at-a-job-for-10-or-more-years*.

2. FutureWorkplace.com, *http://futureworkplace.com/wp-content/uploads/MultipleGenAtWork_infographic.pdf*.

3. Gallup.com, *www.gallup.com/poll/168707/average-retirement-age-rises.aspx*.

4. Jeremy Neuner, "40% of America's Workforce Will Be Freelancers by 2020," Quartz.com, March 20, 2013, *http://qz.com/65279/40-of-americas-workforce-will-be-freelancers-by-2020/*.

Chapter 2

1. All quoted information belongs to Adam Cohen unless otherwise noted. Permission was received to use all material.

2. All quoted information belongs to Melvin Kearney unless otherwise noted. Permission was received to use all material.

3. Bradford Shellhammer quote used with permission.

Chapter 3

1. All quoted information belongs to Gaby Dalkin unless otherwise noted. Permission was received to use all material.

2. Quoted information belongs to Melvin Kearney unless otherwise noted. Permission was received to use all material.

3. Mashable.com, *http://mashable.com/2012/02/01/pinterest-traffic-study/#.xH29b7cEqj*.

4. Christian Guzman, last accessed January 15, 2016, *https://youtube.com/user/Christianguzmanfitne*.

5. Maxx Chewning, last accessed January 15, 2016, *https://youtube.com/user/maxxchewning*.

6. "The Power of Storytelling," Buffer, last accessed January 15, 2016, *http://blog.bufferapp.com/power-of-story*.

7. "Why Every SEO Strategy Needs Infographics," *WMG*, last accessed January 15, 2016, *http://webmarketinggroup.co.uk/why-every-seo-strategy-needs-infographics/*.

8. "What Makes the Perfect Blog Post?" Bit Rebels, last accessed January 15, 2016, *http://bitrebels.com/social/makes-perfect-blog-post-infographic/*.

9. Jeremy Goldman, "The Write Stuff: 8 Steps to the Perfect Blog Post," *Inc.* magazine, *http://inc.com/jeremy-oldman/8-steps-to-creating-the-perfect-blog-post.html*.

10. Ibid.

11. All quoted information belongs to John J. Wall unless otherwise noted. Permission was received to use all material.

12. All quoted information belongs to Jason Miller unless otherwise noted. Permission was received to use all material.

13. "Patreon," *Wikipedia*, last modified December 16, 2015, *http://en.wikipedia.org/wiki/Patreon*.

14. Michael Wolf, "Patreon Seeing Strong Growth in Creators, Pledges, Pageviews," Gigaom.com, *http://research.gigaom.com/2014/02/analysis-patreon-seeing-strong-growth-in-creators-pledges-pageviews/*.

Chapter 4

1. "7 SlideShares to Power Your 2015 Growth," *Firebrand Group*, last accessed January 15, 2016, *www.firebrandgroup.com/7-slideshares-to-power-your-2015-growth/*.

2. "Social Media Business Statistics, Facts, Figures & Trends 2014," *MediaBistro*, last accessed January 15, 2016, *http://mediabistro.com/alltwitter/social-business-trends-2014_b56645*.

3. Jeremy Goldman, "Lessons Learned at Social Fresh EAST 2014," Firebrandgroup.com, *http://firebrandgroup.com/lessons-learned-at-social-fresh-east-2014/*.

4. "Email Etiquette: 10 Simple Rules," *LinkedIn*, *https://linkedin.com/today/post/article/20140427120046-115716357-email-etiquette-10-simple-rules*.

5. "25 Tips for Perfecting Your E-mail Etiquette," *Inc.*, *http://inc.com/guides/2010/06/email-etiquette.html*.

6. "Email Etiquette for Entrepreneurs," *Crew*, *http://blog.pickcrew.com/email-etiquette-for-entrepreneurs/*.

Chapter 6

1. All quoted information belongs to Alyssa Gelbard unless otherwise noted. Permission was received to use all material.

Chapter 8

1. All quoted information belongs to Bradford Shellhammer unless otherwise noted. Permission was received to use all material.

2. Jeremy Goldman, "How Ex-Apple CEO John Sculley Mentors Successful Startups," *Inc., http://inc.com/jeremy-goldman/how-ex-apple-ceo-john-sculley-mentors-successful-startups.html.*

3. Jeremy Goldman, "How to Find and Hire the Next Steve Jobs," *Inc., http://inc.com/jeremy-goldman/how-to-find-and-hire-the-next-steve-jobs.html.*

4. "A Beautiful Smile Makes a Great Impression," HourDetroit.com, *http://hourdetroit.com/Hour-Detroit/March-2013/A-Beautiful-Smile-Makes-a-Great-Impression/.*

5. Peter Economy, "The Hidden Ingredient for a More Productive You (It's Not an App)," Inc-asean.com, *http://inc-asean.com/the-hidden-ingredient-for-a-more-productive-you-its-not-an-app/.*

6. All quoted information belongs to Courtney Spritzer unless otherwise noted. Permission was received to use all material.

7. Jeremy Goldman, "Why Appearances Do Matter (Assuming You Want to Be Successful)," *Inc., http://inc.com/jeremy-goldman/why-appearances-do-matter-assuming-you-want-to-be-successful.html.*

8. Ibid.

9. All quoted information belongs to Alyssa Gelbard unless otherwise noted. Permission was received to use all material.

10. Ted Rubin, "How Crazy Socks Became the Key," Tedrubin.com, *http://tedrubin.com/ how-crazy-socks-became-the-key/*.

11. *https://twitter.com/hashtag/tedsockie*.

12. All quoted information belongs to Sarah Kugelman unless otherwise noted. Permission was received to use all material.

13. All quoted information belongs to Gaby Dalkin unless otherwise noted. Permission was received to use all material.

14. Adam Cohen quote used with permission.

15. Dorie Clark, "Score a Meeting with Just About Anyone," *Harvard Business Review, https://hbr.org/2014/08/ score-a-meeting-with-just-about-anyone/*.

16. All quoted information belongs to Anuj Desai unless otherwise noted. Permission was received to use all material.

Chapter 9

1. All quoted information belongs to Andrea Syrtash unless otherwise noted. Permission was received to use all material.

2. All quoted information belongs to Claudia Lebenthal unless otherwise noted. Permission was received to use all material.

Chapter 10

1. Bradford Shellhammer quote used with permission.

2. All quoted information belongs to Jason Miller unless otherwise noted. Permission was received to use all material.

3. Wanda Thibodeaux, "Individualism in the Workplace," Chron.com, *http://smallbusiness.chron.com/individualism-workplace-13486.html.*

4. "Take This Job and Love It," Pewsocialtrends.com, *www.pewsocialtrends.org/2009/09/17/take-this-job-and-love-it.*

5. Alyssa Gelbard quote used with permission.

6. Sarah Kugelman quote used with permission.

Chapter 11

1. All quoted information belongs to Robert Zimmerman unless otherwise noted. Permission was received to use all material.

2. All quoted information belongs to Gloria Huang unless otherwise noted. Permission was received to use all material.

3. Gaby Dalkin quotes used with permission.

Chapter 12

1. All quoted information belongs to Bradford Shellhammer unless otherwise noted. Permission was received to use all material.

Chapter 13

1. All quoted information belongs to Melvin Kearney unless otherwise noted. Permission was received to use all material.

Chapter 14

1. All quoted information belongs to Andrea Syrtash unless otherwise noted. Permission was received to use all material.

2. All quoted information belongs to Adam Cohen unless otherwise noted. Permission was received to use all material.

Chapter 15

1. Bill Knaus, "Do You Know Why You Still Procrastinate?" *Psychology Today, https:// psychologytoday.com/blog/science-and-sensibility/201409/ do-you-know-why-you-still-procrastinate.*

2. Hara Estroff Marano, "Procrastination: Ten Things to Know," *Psychology Today, http://psychologytoday.com/ articles/200308/procrastination-ten-things-know.*

3. Donald P. Moynihan, Thomas DeLeire, and Kohei Enami, "A Life Worth Living" (abstract), *The American Review of Public Administration, http://arp.sagepub.com/ content/45/3/311.abstract.*

4. Jacquelyn Smith, "How Much Coworker Socializing Is Good for Your Career?" Forbes.com, *http://forbes. com/sites/jacquelynsmith/2013/09/24/how-much-coworker- socializing-is-good-for-your-career/#y6c827fd5956.*

5. Andrew J. Oswald, Eugenio Proto, and Daniel Sgroi, *Happiness and Productivity, https://www2.warwick. ac.uk/fac/soc/economics/staff/eproto/workingpapers/ happinessproductivity.pdf.*

6. "How to Be Happier at Work," Happify.com, *www. happify.com/hd/happiness-at-work-infographic/?srid=hfp.*

7. *https://aabacosmallbusiness.com/advisor/be-true-to-yourself- and-say-not-interview-with-greg-mckeown-205152668.html.*

8. Gaby Dalkin quote used with permission.

9. Jeremy Goldman, "How to Find and Hire the Next Steve Jobs," *Inc.*, *http://inc.com/jeremy-goldman/how-to-find-and-hire-the-next-steve-jobs.html*.

10. All quoted information belongs to Jess Davis unless otherwise noted. Permission was received to use all material.

Index

About the Authors

About the Authors

Jeremy Goldman

For more than 15 years, Jeremy Goldman has been working with companies looking to take their digital marketing to the next level. He has managed ecommerce and social media for a number of global beauty brands, including Kiehl's Since 1851. Jeremy is the founder and CEO of Firebrand Group, an award-winning futureproofing firm focused on building powerful brands through innovative digital marketing and social media strategies, and has counted Unilever, L'Oreal, Consumer Reports, Colgate, Amtrak, and Movado amongst his clientele.

Jeremy is a recognized branding expert, and has been featured in the *Wall Street Journal*, BBC, Mashable, CNBC, SmartMoney, Workforce.com, ReadWriteWeb, Clickz, and InformationWeek. *Business Insider* calls him "one of the 25 Most Influential Ad Execs On Twitter."

In addition to his work managing Firebrand Group, Jeremy is the founder of Mosaic, a New York City–based networking group helping digital marketers at all levels work on their personal brands. He is a columnist for Inc.com, a regular contributor to *Harvard Business Review*, and enjoys spending at least three minutes daily with his wife, daughter, and five pets.

Ali B. Zagat

A seasoned writer and content strategist, Ali got her start in the publishing industry as an editor at Thomson Reuters. She started writing digital and social media content for independent designers and discovered a talent for connecting boutique brands with their target audiences. This led to work with etailers, such as cult favorite perfume house Black Phoenix Alchemy Lab, and spearheading sales and product copy for high-end and niche designer goods at the fast-paced startup Fab.com. She helped develop Fab's blog strategy to speak to the multifaceted interests of a design lover, and created some of the site's highest-ever trafficked pieces.

Ali added some strategic and analytic tools to her professional kit as a member of the managing editorial team at Amazon, where she helped teams on both coasts drive a number of key initiatives to optimize communication and set plans for achieving their long-term goals. Currently a copywriter for branding agency 160over90, Ali helped Jeremy prepare his first book, *Going Social*, for publication. With the philosophy that every brand can and should create opportunities to reach out to prospective fans and have meaningful conversations with its existing user base, Ali creates digital and social content and content strategies for partners including Birchbox, Edible Brooklyn, Dwell, Creed, Rodale's, Anthropologie, Fit Bottomed Girls, and ALOHA. She lives in Philadelphia with her adorable husband and newborn daughter.